MW00736850

Inside the Cup

ALI –
BEST WISHES &
enjoy THS STARBUCKS' –

– Kany B

Inside the Cup

By

Kenneth Brown

INSIDE THE CUP

© 2012 Kenneth Brown

All rights reserved.

No part of this book may be reproduced in any form or by any electronic or mechanical means including information storage and retrieval systems, or transmitted, in any form or by any means (electronic, mechanical, photocopying, recording, or otherwise), without permission in writing from the author and the publisher. The only exception is by a reviewer, who may quote short excerpts in a published review.

The scanning, uploading, and distribution of this book via the Internet or via any other means without the permission of the publisher is illegal and punishable by law. Please purchase only authorized electronic editions and do not participate in or encourage electronic piracy of copyrightable materials. Your support of the author's rights is appreciated.

The information presented herein represents the views of the author as of the date of publication. This book is presented for informational purposes only. Due to the rate at which conditions change, the author reserves the right to alter and update his opinions at any time. While every attempt has been made to verify the information in this book, the author does not assume any responsibility for errors, inaccuracies, or omissions.

Cover and interior design by Kenneth Brown, Fee Publishing.

Published by

Fee Publishing

Boston, MA 02120

ISBN 978-0-9852408-0-6

LCCN 2012933919

For more information visit www.insidethecupbook.com.

Printed in the United States of America

First Edition 2012

Contents

Frozen Beverages

Acknowledgements

Thanks to...

Linda Krol, for pushing all of the right buttons to get me to thrive in my position and for constantly encouraging me day in and day out.

All of the managers and directors who played a part in my training and development.

The hundreds of partners with whom I've worked in the Boston and New York areas for forging a story with me.

The countless customers who let me into their lives and allowed me to share a few minutes of their day with them, every day.

My friend Sarah, for introducing me to Starbucks as a customer way back in the day.

The businesses, schools, and organizations in the South Shore, Massachusetts area that made it possible for my stores to make a difference in the local community.

The partners in the Cohasset and Hingham stores who made going to work each and every day pure joy.

And above all, to my lovely wife Ashley for giving me the support and love that I needed to see this book through.

Foreword

Often people correlate working at Starbucks with making coffee, sampling pastries, and talking with regular customers all day. That is certainly a part of the day-to-day activity, but there is also a lot of not-so-glamorous work to do. Managers at Starbucks are responsible for much more than writing schedules and training employees to serve coffee. In addition to being trained in Situation Leadership and Retail Management, they are also usually experts in everything coffee— from how the bean is grown, to how it should be ground for your specific coffee machine, and everything in between.

Early in my career I went through the Starbucks management training program and was lucky enough to have Kenneth Brown as not only my Store Manager but also my mentor, as I learned everything there was to know about the coffee business. Since I've moved on to a career in Business Marketing & Communications, there have been many times when I've been able to reference the leadership, business management, and customer service experience that I gained during my time at Starbucks. But for many former Starbucks managers and baristas, it is our knowledge of the Starbucks culture and language that most people are interested in.

Of course, all industries have their own jargon, often with dozens of acronyms that were created in an attempt to simplify company philosophies. But Starbucks takes its jargon to the next level, to its own language. Starbucks' unique language can intimidate and perplex even the most savvy of coffee connoisseurs. Many customers have been able to figure out that *tall* means *small* and *grande* means *medium*— it's even been joked about in several movies and TV shows. But do you know what SFV or PSL stand for?

Starbucks baristas are trained in dozens of different acronyms, using them for everything from the codes on the sides of your cup, to explaining how their farmers grow their coffee beans. To keep things fun in the store, some of the baristas and I used to try speaking to each other in code. We'd call out drinks to each other in only the codes that are written on the cup, and see how long we could go speaking in Starbucks acronyms.

"I want a triple tall, 2p SFV, N, XF, 180°, No WC, PSL."

Could you follow that? Probably only if you've worked at a Starbucks or are a super-regular customer. It might have been fun for a bunch of baristas trying to practice the code, but anyone who overheard these conversations was likely to be completely lost. I'll never forget Kenny's reaction when he first heard one of these conversations. He laughed and looked at us like we were speaking Latin. "What are you talking about?" he said trying to hide a smile. "Why can't you just make it simple and say what it is?"

It is that need to keep things simple, combined with his expert knowledge of coffee and Starbucks culture, which makes Kenny the perfect person to author this book. This book is a great reference guide to help customers or newbies decipher the complexities of the Starbucks language. Of course, with the dozens of different ways to customize a drink, the possibilities are limitless and would be difficult to include in a reasonably sized book. But Kenny does a great job of deciphering the basics and giving his readers a great foundation on which to build your own coffee knowledge.

Whether you want to learn how to customize a specific drink to your own unique perfection, or want to venture out of your comfort zone and try something new, this book will give you a great place to start. Keep it handy any time you visit a store, and you'll be on your way to becoming a Starbucks aficionado!

Now if you'll excuse me, I've got a craving for a quad grande, nonfat, extra foam, upside-down, caramel macchiato (*See page 114 if you're curious*).

Marceline Randall

Marketing Communications Manager/Consultant,
former Starbucks Manager, and PSL lover!

How to Read This Book

Sometimes opening a new book may seem daunting. This may be because of the subject matter, the length, or simply because we feel compelled to take in the book in its entirety. Due to the nature of this book I don't expect everyone to read it cover to cover. My hope is that some will. I think there is something to be said and something to be gained by doing that. I have structured this book so that there is a certain progression to it, especially in the first half where each chapter builds upon the previous one.

At the same time you can jump in at "your drink." I've also structured this book to be a quick reference guide, or "how to modify" resource, that you can keep at your disposal. This is to make your Starbucks experience more satisfying. For this reason I've tried to optimize it for ease of use. It's also my hope that when you're about to visit Starbucks, or while you're waiting in the drive-thru (not sure that I want to encourage people to read while they're in the drive-thru, but I will anyway), that you'll be able to use it to modify the beverage of your choice to your liking. Since I tried to structure this book for ease of use you might find some small repetitions if you read it cover to cover. Forgive me if you do.

By nature Starbucks is an ever-changing enterprise. For that reason they have products that come and go over time. You may find that a longtime favorite beverage of yours has been removed from the menu only to have a new one replace it. With this in mind I've tried to keep this book focused mostly on those drinks that are staples on the menu. That is, they're highly likely to always be part of the menu.

Also, there are many popular beverages that are seasonal. I've taken the time to write about them because of their popularity. However, I've also been sure to point out that they're seasonal, along with their season, to dispel any confusion.

I hope that you'll use this book to branch out and try drinks aside from what you normally order or maybe even try your first drink ever. I hope that it piques your interests and raises your spirits. I'll be very pleased if it can enhance not only your time with family, friends, and coworkers but also your alone time. If it can alleviate some anxiety when ordering, that'll be good too.

If you enjoy it I hope that you will share your enjoyment with others. If you're reading this because it has been shared with you then I guess this book has already begun to serve its purpose.

There are so many heartwarming, funny, and crazy stories that revolve around partner and customer experiences that I have decided to follow this book with another that is dedicated to those experiences. If you would like to share your story in this book then I invite you to submit it on at www.InsideTheCupBook.com.

Introduction

What is the Aim of This Book?

We all know the scenario. A man entering Starbucks for the very first time steps up to the counter. He surveys the menu. Overwhelmed and intimidated, he breaks into a cold, sweaty panic. He does not want to hold up the line. "I'll just take a small coffee," he blurts out with a surrendering tone.

The barista asks, "What kind of coffee would you like? Bold? Mild?"

Not sure about the difference, and already bewildered by the aura of "dark Starbucks coffee," the man says, "Mild."

The barista repeats back, "Tall mild coffee."

"No wait, I want a *small* coffee," the man insists.

"Yes, I know. Tall mild."

"No, *small*." The man wonders if this is not some sort of bizarre initiation prank.

"No sir, you really do mean tall. At Starbucks, tall is small."

Mission accomplished. The man will grudgingly take his coffee and flee from the store. He is thoroughly confused and might never visit Starbucks again. On top of that he'll comment to friends and family about how he was in Starbucks the other day and had no idea what anything was. How the barista, partner, employee, or whatever you call them, argued with him and tried to get him to buy a larger size.

This is about the time that his friend, a regular Starbucks customer, chimes in with her two cents and says, "Well, I always get my triple grande, nonfat, no-foam, upside-down Caramel Macchiato." Yeah, that didn't help. If you're not a regular Starbucks customer then you know what that does to you when you hear it. It makes you terminate the conversation.

The man will say how he just wants a cup of coffee. He can't understand why anyone visits Starbucks because it's so confusing and uncomfortable. He doesn't understand it so he thinks it's not for him.

In actuality he hasn't been informed enough to make a decision.

Is that what Starbucks is about? Being hoity-toity or part of the "in-crowd"? Is it an exclusive club? Is it not for people who just want a cup of coffee?

Well, just to confuse you more, the answer is *yes* and *no* at the same time. It really is for everyone. If you want "just a cup of coffee," then it's for you. If you want to be a coffee connoisseur or part of a cultural phenomenon, then it's for you as well. If you want to grab-and-get on your way to work or hang in the café it's for you.

Before I go any further, let me make one thing clear. I'm not here to promote or scorn the coffee maker. I'm here to simply offer a service: access to my knowledge of the menu. This is to help those who are intimidated by the menu, embarrassed to order, afraid to order, sent to Starbucks with a list of drinks that you can't pronounce, looking to increase your Starbucks knowledge, or just curious about all of those crazy drinks. Maybe you don't know what a cappuccino, latte, Americano, doppio, and macchiato are. Maybe you just want to learn how to pronounce those words. Or, perhaps, you simply want to know a little more about Starbucks because our society is fascinated with it.

I've always felt that one of the greatest obstacles for customers and potential customers is that they don't understand the drinks. They don't truly understand what Starbucks is offering. They're uninformed and, in some cases, misinformed.

My aim is to better inform you so you can decide if you want to be a customer or not; if you want a latte, Americano, drip coffee, or nothing at all. And I'll even throw in a few entertaining stories along the way. I don't want to push you in any direction. I just want you to be able to make a decision in a comfortable and relaxing environment, not in an awkward and hurried manner at the counter with everybody staring at you.

Because I worked at Starbucks I get sprinkled with questions from family, friends, and anyone who knows I worked there. What is a ____? What's in a ____? When I go in and say, "____," are you guys thinking "____"? It's always the same questions. What's a partner? How do you remember all of those drinks? How do you remember my drink? You probably drink a lot of coffee, huh? I'm going to try to answer most of those questions.

This book is about customer and partner interaction. How it works on the Starbucks end and how you can feel more comfortable on your end. You'll learn how to speak Starbucks, so to speak. So sit back and enjoy. Hopefully you'll learn what that machiatty whatever thing is and discover something that you like.

Why Did I Choose the Title That I Did?

When trying to decide on a title for this book, I constructed a whole list of potential candidates. The list ranged from the corny *(Cup, Smell, Slurp)* to the clever *(Caffeinated)*. I almost settled on *Gergo*. What the heck is that? It means *lingo* in Italian. I'm really glad I decided against it. It would've just made everything more confusing. How ironic that would've been. So, *Inside the Cup* won out.

There is a meaning behind the title besides the obvious play on words. While *Inside the Cup: Translating Starbucks Into a Drinkable Language* will primarily serve you when ordering beverages, it will also give you a global understanding of Starbucks and the partner-customer relationship. Enhancing that understanding will increase the joy you experience upon each visit.

A large part of this book will reveal how you can make the most of your customer experience at Starbucks. However, I believe that calling it a "how-to" book would be misleading and do the book a disservice. Hopefully it will not only teach you how to choose and modify your favorite beverages but also how to enjoy the many Starbucks offerings for all that they are intended.

Why Write the Chapters that I Did?

In my time at Starbucks I heard the same questions asked again and again by customers. I also saw the same breakdowns between Starbucks and those customers again and again. Outside of Starbucks I was asked the same questions over and over by anyone who knew I worked there. It's these topics that I have tried to address as I wrote this book.

Here are the six questions most frequently posed.

1) How can I modify my drink so that I will enjoy it more?

This question is answered by the larger part of the book. Many customers order the same drink day after day after day. They like it so they stick with it. Then, one day, they overhear another customer order soy milk, or sugar free syrup, or a specific temperature. Until that moment they never knew those options were available. They probably knew they could modify their drink some way but maybe not in those specific ways.

Hopefully, after reading this book, you will enjoy a beverage that you have tailored exactly to suit your desires.

2) What else might I like?

I bet close to 90% of Starbucks customers get the exact same drink every single time. They love it and that's great. Some of those customers are well educated about the menu, but many of them don't know the menu aside from their drink. They either stick with a drink they find, because that's simple and easy, or they're too embarrassed to ask questions about other items. Many times customers do ask questions about other items or say that they would like to try other drinks. Either way, the barrier between that thought and actually trying something new is the inability to take that leap of faith for a drink they don't know.

Hopefully this book will turn you on to some beverages that you haven't tried before by breaking down that barrier.

3) Why does Starbucks have this different language that I don't understand?

The vocabulary used at Starbucks is foreign to just about everyone who doesn't work there. When I started working at Starbucks I didn't know anything about coffee or espresso, much less dolce latte. The gap in vocabulary between the baristas and the customers standing across the counter can be immense. Hopefully the chapters in this book, and the glossary at the end, will help narrow that gap for you.

4) I'd love to work at Starbucks. Can you get me a job there?

I wish I had a dollar for every time I heard this one. People seem to have this fascination with working at Starbucks. I've always thought it was funny. Even when I applied to work there I didn't have the same fascination. Well, not in the same context as those who speak to me about it. I was interested in the business model.

The big fascination is with making drinks. But hold your horses before you apply. There's a lot more to the job than just whipping up drinks for people. On top of that there are a lot of applicants, creating fierce competition. To help shed some light on what is needed to get hired and succeed at Starbucks, I added a bonus chapter at the end titled *How to Get Hired at Starbucks.*

5) Who are Starbucks customers, anyway?

Starbucks and its customers carry a certain connotation with them. Just for fun, I start the book with *Customers* to take a look at the different categories of customers that frequent the stores. Where do you fit in?

6) Where does the coffee come from?

In an environment like Starbucks, where the product offering is an enigma to many, you field a lot of questions. As a manager, you get even more. Every day we would get dozens of questions about brewing, sourcing, caffeine content, coffee descriptions, food pairings, and more. I don't expect to answer all of those questions in this book but hopefully I can answer a majority of them. The *Coffee*, *Tea*, and *Caffeine* chapters should help deepen your knowledge of those topics.

Starbucks is Hard Work

My years at Starbucks were challenging. Just like any job there were ups and downs. I worked with a lot of great people that I had to say 'bye to. There were also times that I had the inglorious task of terminating someone. In between those two things were hiring shortages, sales goals, product launches, community events, scheduling dilemmas, emergencies, thefts, great partner performances, holiday seasons, a myriad of performance reports and reviews, and uplifting and disappointing interactions with partners and customers alike. Every day was different and surprising. Sometimes my team and I excelled and sometimes we failed. It's a fast-paced job that requires an inordinate amount of meticulous multitasking and foresight.

It takes a special kind of person to be able to work at Starbucks and perform well. You need to be truly ceaseless to stay on top of everything. A lot of different skill sets are needed. I worked with a lot of special people over the years. It is my personal hope that through this book you will gain a greater understanding of, and respect for, your local baristas. Who knows, after reading this, maybe you'll become inspired to be one.

Just for the Record

As the author of this book, I don't represent Starbucks. It's written entirely under my own volition. For that reason you're getting my opinions and not verified company statements.

For the same reason, I can't guarantee that everything in this book is 100% accurate. I believe it is, at least at the time I wrote it. Certainly I was in a position to be able to intelligently speak about the things that I have. It's quite possible that you'll be reading this a year or two after I wrote it and find some small detail that Starbucks has changed. I tried to write about the mainstays for that reason. The majority of Starbucks' products form a core that doesn't change while on the fringe there are a few that come and go. This book is about the North American core. If you believe you've found a contradiction or inaccuracy somewhere, then you should check with your local Starbucks to clarify. Keep these points in mind as you read.

Chapter One:

Customers

"If it weren't for the caffeine I'd have no personality whatsoever."
– Anonymous

Starbucks customers are a special breed. You understand this whether you're a customer or not. If you are, then you know how you are when you visit Starbucks. You have to have your drink just so and if you don't get it, well, we won't talk about that.

If you're not a customer then you've still, undoubtedly, spoken with those who are and know what they are like. You're also probably aware of the stereotype that has been bestowed upon Starbucks customers by the media and the masses. You know – the pretentious, high spending, spoiled, caffeine addicted automatons that we all are.

Not so fast. I don't think that's entirely accurate. Sure, a lot of us are addicted to caffeine, $4 lattes can be expensive if you have to have them three times a day, and many of us do want what we want; but pretentious? I don't think so. Besides, customers don't fit into a neat little stereotype because we're all different. We're all individuals visiting Starbucks for our own reasons.

So who are Starbucks customers? I've identified ten different quirky and amusing categories of people that I've seen on a regular basis – my own stereotypes, if you will. You might not fit into one of them but there's a really good chance that you do. You may even fit into a couple of them.

The Starbucks Maven

Have you ever met someone who knows everything about a particular topic? Italian wine, *Star Wars*, the 1963 World Series, or whatever it is? I'm talking in a freakish kind of way. If they were on *Jeopardy*, and their special topic was a category, you know they'd be cleaning house.

Mavens aren't only knowledgeable about *their* topic; they're savvy about it. One spring day, when I lived on the South Shore of Massachusetts, I wanted to buy a new car. While speaking with the car salesman I soon realized that I was speaking with a maven. Not about cars though. This guy was a different kind of maven. He knew everything about *deals* on the South Shore.

He'd say "Now, the Clarion Hotel serves warm chocolate chip cookies in the lobby on Wednesdays at 2pm…Sunday afternoons Joe's restaurant has free wings in the bar lounge. I used to go down there every week….if you take the ferry on Sunday mornings they only charge you half price." I listened intently as this guy laid down unadvertised deal after unadvertised deal in the local area. Forget the car. What hotel has free cookies? Where are the best priced chili dogs? This guy was a maven of deals. Too bad he didn't tell me where the best deal for my car was.

Mavens know everything about their topic. They're connoisseurs. Although many customers would like to think that they're mavens, there are very few who actually are. To be honest with you, if they're not a former partner, I have no idea how they know this much about Starbucks. You might be tempted to call it an obsession or a fascination. I suppose it is.

Mavens are generally every day customers, have read all of the Starbucks books, keep up to date on Starbucks news, and ask the partners lots of questions. Some own stock and many have a friend working for Starbucks. They're usually pleasant to speak with.

If there's a breakdown somewhere in a maven's knowledge it usually comes within a specific product offering. There might be a pastry or a piece of merchandise that they're unaware of, but they usually know more than the average barista about what's happening with the company from a macro perspective. I'd find myself learning from mavens who visited the store. They'd leave and I'd think to myself, "How come I didn't know about that?"

Partners

One day a customer comes into the store and orders an iced, quad, tall, one pump raspberry, four pumps Classic, nonfat, three melted raw sugar, shaken latte. Whoa. Hold everything. Something is amiss. Customers don't order drinks like that. That drink doesn't even make sense. Sure enough that customer is actually a partner in disguise, visiting on vacation.

As you may imagine, partners and former partners are avid customers. Most were customers before they were partners. Some are even mavens. There is one thing that is readily identifiable with a partner. It's that they really know how to make a drink and they're particular about it. Not particular like customers, particular like partners.

When a partner comes into the store and orders you know immediately that they're a partner. The first clue is that they order their drink with a million different modifiers. The second is that they order obscure modifications. Many times they're modifications that I've never heard ordered. You can only come up with modifications like this if you've had the opportunity to endlessly experiment with making drinks. The third clue is that they order it perfectly and without hesitation. By speaking their modifications in the correct order, and with fluidity, they're way too polished to have never worked at Starbucks. It's a dead giveaway.

Let me give you another example. Sometimes I like to have a Coffee Frappuccino. For me, the standard recipe is too thick and too sweet. To modify both of those this is what I order: decaf, tall, milk to the top line, smoothie size scoop of ice, one pump of base, in a grande cup, Coffee Frappuccino. Ahhh, just the way I like it. I'm always pegged as a partner when I'm in a new store. Customers don't order their drinks like that. Well, maybe you will after reading this book.

You're going to read about, or have read about, all of the modifications that I list and recommend. With those in mind, come back to this and you'll better understand what I'm talking about.

Buddy-Buddy

Some partners and customers go fishing together, some share books, others take yoga classes together, and some babysit for each other. Heck, I even invited customers to my wedding.

Many customers are real buddy-buddy with the partners. When

you're working at Starbucks you get to know some of the regulars really well. You even become friends with them. It's a risky proposition for store business because the friendship could always have a falling out. At the same time, that's life. So I embraced it.

Every store has at least twenty customers who know every partner by name. Everyone is happy to see them and anxious to chat with them. It always seems that there's so much to talk about when they visit. That's because they share their lives with you. They don't see the partners as just another bunch of employees at another place of business. They see them as friends. They often hang out and talk about topics that go far beyond your average chit-chat. Since many customers are in the store every day, and many partners work there for years, strong friendships develop naturally. Many of these people, and the daily interactions with them, are a part of who, and what, I miss most about working at Starbucks. In my mind's eye I can still picture regular customers walking into the store and being greeted: "Norm!"

Mom

Many times a vehicle would pull up to the drive-thru speaker and there it was: a car full of screaming kids.

"I want a Frappuccino!"

"I want chocolate milk!"

"Can we get cookies?"

Now don't get me wrong, I love kids. But I was also happy that I wasn't on the other side of that speaker. When they would pull up to the window all I could do was laugh and offer my condolences. Mom obviously has her hands full today.

Moms are a big part of the customer base. Usually they visit the store at lunchtime or right after school gets out. They often visit the drive-thru, because it's easier, but sometimes they can be seen pushing their strollers inside Starbucks' shoebox-sized stores.

I have this mental image forever ingrained in my mind of a mom, in her van, reaching back to deal with her raucous kids. To this day I still laugh when I think about that.

Here's what I think happens. Mom, and sometimes dad, has responsibility for the kids; but she has to have her Starbucks. Maybe they're at home and she loads everybody in the car, or maybe she's just picking them up from school. Whatever it is, they've made their way to Starbucks.

At this point it's hard not to buy them something. That's part of the deal, isn't it? "Be good and I'll get you something." Yeah, it doesn't always work.

I couldn't always see into the back of the van so I didn't always know how many kids were actually in there. Sometimes it seemed like I was passing an endless parade of drinks out the window, just wondering where they were all going. There must've been a soccer team in there or something.

Other times mom was dead silent as the kids screamed away. She'd given up. I could see the look of defeat on her face. She silently paid, took the drinks, and passed them into the back of the vehicle without ever looking. You can only smile at that. If you're a parent then you've probably been there.

This was a far more common occurrence in the drive-thru than in the café. Kids who are in the café are usually better behaved. I guess if your kid is a little out of control on that day then you usually won't bring them inside. I can't say I blame you.

Mr. / Ms. Exact Change

Have you ever been standing in line and seen the customer in front of you approach the counter, immediately hand over their money, take their drink, and leave? No words were spoken except "Thank you." You marvel at what just took place. Before you even order you have to ask the barista, "Who was that guy?" Obviously he has to be someone important.

The barista tells you, "Oh, that was just John. He gets the same thing every day and always pays with the exact change. He's usually in a hurry so we prepare his drink as soon as we see him walk in."

The morning is the busiest time for most stores. It's also when customers are in the biggest hurry. Many will craft their visit so that it's as time efficient as possible. They do that by getting the same drink every day, employing minimal, or in some cases zero, conversation, and paying with exact change. Because their beverage is always the same, it's constructed as soon as they're spotted. If it costs $3.52, then every day they pass exactly $3.52 across the counter.

They're a well oiled machine. They're efficient by their own standards and a pleasure to the customers in line behind them, as they keep the line moving fast.

Sometimes that $3.52 is the only cash they're carrying. So when price changes take effect, everything stops. Sometimes they don't have enough to pay. Of course, they'll always be notified of the price change and then considered paid in full. Nevertheless, it's awkward to stop a well oiled machine.

Classic Guy

I can still remember the first day he came in. He set two Harley Davidson to-go cups on the counter and from behind his dark sunglasses and leather jacket said, "Fill 'em up." I filled them right to the top. When I put the lids on the coffee spilled down the sides. I can still picture him saying to me "I don't care. I like 'm like that." He walked out of the store, got on his bike, and was gone. Classic.

I call this category *Classic Guy* because it's almost exclusively men who occupy it. They come into the store almost every day. They're the kind of guy who's a real man's man. They almost don't even want to admit that they go to Starbucks because their manly friends may poke fun at them. They counter that by stating that they come in for the bold coffee. Of course they do. They might add cream and sugar but many times they take it black. They don't want anything to do with lattes, Frappuccinos, or any drink that they consider to be "foo-foo."

When asked about any of those drinks they respond, "I don't know anything about that other stuff," or "I don't like that other crap. Just give me the high-test." I love those guys. Many times they don't even care what coffee you give them. The just want coffee.

Before working at Starbucks I was one of them. But over the course of five years I've slowly broken down. Today, I drink as many "foo-foo" drinks as I do drip coffees.

The Runner

Some customers aren't customers at all. They're sent to get drinks for someone else. I like to call them *runners*. When they approach the counter they usually say something like, "Here are some drinks.

I don't know what they are," as they hand over a list. Sometimes they don't say anything. It's kind of like they're spellbound.

I can almost hear a barista shouting across the store, "We've got a list!"

The truth is there are two different kinds of runners. There are those who are regular customers themselves and those who have never stepped foot inside a Starbucks except as a runner. The two couldn't be more opposite.

The former kind of runner is high energy and employs sales skills. They're a commander of sorts. They may have volunteered to pick up the drinks for the office, hair salon, or wherever they came from. You can picture them persuading their friends and colleagues to buy a drink. "Starbucks is great. I can't believe you've never had it. You know what you should try? Get a ..." Then they'll turn their attention to the next person – "What are you getting?" It's a caffeinated conversation.

Once, a movie was being filmed down the street from my store. A runner from the crew would come in and get twenty or thirty drinks for her coworkers. You have to be a commander to pull off a list like that.

The latter kind of runner delivers their list with great trepidation. I feel for these individuals. They must feel like a lamb in the lion's den. They just hand over their list and pay, afraid to even speak. They don't normally get a drink for themselves. More often than not, while they're waiting for their drinks, they'll ask something like, "So what's in a cappuccino anyway?" I've tried to offer free drinks to them but they don't usually bite. They might not have a list for a group of people. Many times it'll be a husband picking up his wife's drink.

High School Kids

High school kids. They're hyper, loud, and travel in packs. It's not an issue, but I'm just saying. You know how they, or you, are. We've all been there. I think when the final bell rings they pack into the car of the kid who has a driver's license and race off to ransack the local Starbucks.

On the flip side, they make a good recruiting pool. Many are passionate customers who have an interest in becoming baristas as well. I've had many competent high school kids work with me.

Now, I said that they travel in packs. That doesn't mean that they all order drinks. If there's a group of five then maybe two or three of them will order. Some don't have any money and some borrow from their friends. "You can have my lunch tomorrow." They scrap together $4 just so they can come in with their friends and get a Frappuccino. Ahhh, those were the days.

That's the other thing: they love Frappuccinos. Every weekday afternoon from two to four o'clock is Frappuccino mania. Starting in the springtime, and especially when Starbucks runs its Frappy Hour promotion, it can get so busy that it's almost unbearable. And it's mostly high school kids. Three or four groups of three or four high school kids ordering Frappuccinos can put a lot of stress on the partners who are working. Frappuccinos aren't easy to make and, in quantities like that, things can bottleneck in a hurry.

High school kids only drink three things: Frappuccinos, sweetened iced teas, and sometimes hot chocolates. These kids love the sweet stuff. That's why they like these drinks. Most of them haven't developed a palate for coffee yet. I guess that comes during college.

Regulars

Most customers are regulars. They visit Starbucks on some kind of a regular basis. That could be three times per week or three times per day. However often it is, these customers are the ones who make up the vast majority of Starbucks' business.

Some regulars like to think that they're unique because they visit Starbucks every day. For some it's a matter of pride. I've never had the courage to tell them that most customers are regulars. Partners get close with regulars and therefore tend to get possessive of their relationships. I would visit other stores and see some of my regulars there. "You're cheating on me?" I would quip.

For some customers Starbucks is a luxury; for regulars it's a necessity. In fact, there's another name for regulars: addicts. Don't deny it. It's caffeine people. I say that with all of the love in the world. Most will admit that they have some form of an addiction to their drink. It might be the caffeine, the sugar, or maybe the social interaction that happens when visiting the store. Some are simply addicted to their routine. Without it, their whole day is thrown off. But most come for the caffeine.

Regulars get the same drink most of the time, if not all of the time. They may or may not know a lot about the menu but they certainly know "their drink." They have to have it to function. I once had a customer who liked her drink with twelve Splendas. She wanted to cut back so she started getting eleven and a half. She was serious.

Another lady was so addicted to caffeine, and Starbucks, that she would sneak VIA instant coffee packets into her religious retreat, where caffeine wasn't allowed. She said the packets were just the right size for this covert operation.

At one store we had a large clientele of au pairs. They would come in at different times with their host families. During the same period we also had a Wednesday night knitting circle. On any given Wednesday evening there would be seven to twenty knitters who would gather for a couple hours of socializing and knitting. One fateful Wednesday evening, more than twenty au pairs decided to have a meeting at Starbucks. I'll leave the ensuing melee to your imagination.

Avid Customer

Once I was helping a customer and noticed, out of the corner of my eye, that she had a peculiar handbag. Upon further inspection I realized that it was entirely made out of Starbucks gift cards. Wow. Not only did this lady need to be crafty to pull this off, she had to be an avid customer.

Some customers love Starbucks so much that they have to have everything Starbucks. They only drink Starbucks coffee, collect Starbucks mugs and Bearistas (don't ask), their coffee or espresso maker has to be Starbucks, and the perfect gift for their friend just happens to be from Starbucks. Maybe you've received one.

Avid customers have a real affinity for merchandise. They love to collect items. The most popular collectibles are certainly the Starbucks city mugs – mugs with pictures of cities from all over the world. Bearistas are a popular collectible as well. Okay, okay, I'll explain them. They're simply stuffed bears that come in various themes, such as Halloween, Christmas, or Valentine's Day.

Outside of the holiday season Starbucks doesn't sell a whole lot of merchandise. However, a large chunk of what it does sell is purchased by avid customers.

These customers certainly drive a lot of business for Starbucks. That's not only because they spend more but because they act as spokespeople. They talk about how much they like the brand and you see it when visiting their homes. When speaking with avid customers I picture a room in their home with vast shelving that contains bearista... after bearista... after bearista.

Chapter Two:

Coffee

"I never drink coffee at lunch. I find it keeps me awake for the afternoon." – Ronald Reagan

"In Seattle you haven't had enough coffee until you can thread a sewing machine while it's still running." – Jeff Bezos

Every year, over seven million tons of coffee are produced worldwide. From that Americans consume more than 146 billion cups. Yeah, it's a good business to be in. But how does it work, where does it come from, what's the best way to brew it, and what are the differences between coffees?

Coffee is cultivated in more than fifty countries all along the equatorial line. That's where the climate is perfect for coffee plants to thrive. That's why Maine isn't known for its coffee fields. In fact, Hawaii and Puerto Rico are the only places where coffee is grown in the United States. Most of those seven million tons are picked by hand in South America, Africa, and Southeast Asia. Brazil is the world's largest producer.

There are two common species of coffee plants: arabica and canephora. The most common form of canephora is robusta. So it's arabica and robusta that you usually hear about. Arabica plants generally grow at higher elevations, are more difficult to grow, and yield less than robusta plants. They take years to produce berries and are very susceptible to weather changes (frost will destroy them). However, they're considered the superior of the two because their flavors are more vibrant and complex. Robusta plants, on the other hand, aren't as delicate, yield a greater volume, and are simply more economical. They're more bitter than Arabica plants.

But don't write robusta coffee off just yet. Many excellent coffees incorporate it to some degree. In fact, it's really what has allowed coffee to be affordable; to become a commodity. With that said, Starbucks uses arabica beans. Are you really surprised? I didn't think so. They want to use the best beans possible. And, as you've probably guessed, arabica beans are more expensive because of their delicate and tasty nature. Starbucks likes to use the cream of the crop, so to speak.

Arabica beans are most commonly found in western South America, eastern Africa, and some islands in Indonesia. So guess where Starbucks purchases most of its coffee. Exactly. Those places.

The coffee beans are picked by hand, processed by either the dry or wet processing method, and bagged. Details of the processing methods are beyond the scope of this book but essentially they rip the bean out of the berry, wash it, and then dry it. Once the coffee beans arrive at Starbucks roasting plants (Seattle, WA; Carson City, NV; York, PA; and Columbia, SC) they're then roasted according to secret recipes and packaged.

Sounds pretty straightforward, doesn't it? But what do you do with it once you get it? That's where the four fundamentals come in.

Four Fundamentals

When preparing coffee it's critical to follow the four fundamentals that lead to a perfect cup: freshness, grind, water, and proportion. Just as important is following them consistently each time so that you can come to appreciate and enjoy all that the coffee has to offer.

1. Freshness

It's important to use fresh coffee. If you don't then you'll risk losing the best features of it. Unopened, Starbucks coffee will stay fresh for months in its FlavorLock bag. The bag has a one-way valve that allows carbon dioxide to escape but doesn't allow oxygen to enter. Once the bag is opened the coffee will remain at peak freshness for about a week. After a week the quality begins to diminish. You can keep the coffee in the bag but the best thing to do is transfer it into an airtight container. That'll preserve it longer.

I always get asked by customers if they should freeze their coffee. The answer is no. Freezing does bad things. First, it breaks down the flavorful oils that manifest themselves when the coffee is roasted. Your coffee won't taste right. Second, coffee soaks up what's around it because it's porous. Do you see where I'm going with this? If you have salmon in your freezer you will also have... Salmon Blend! I've never seen Salmon Blend in a store so I'm guessing it isn't any good. I've also never seen coffee in the freezer section.

Grinding only what you need to brew at the moment is another way to preserve freshness. It reduces the amount of air contact.

To sum up, the best thing you can do is open your coffee, place it in an airtight container, grind only what you're going to be brewing at that time, never put it in the freezer, and drink it regularly.

2. Grind

How do I grind my coffee? That's an important question when you're about to brew. If you're having your coffee ground in the store, or you're purchasing coffee for someone else, then you need to know this at the time of purchase.

It's important for the grind to be accurate or it can change your coffee experience altogether. Ground too fine and the coffee will either be too strong or it will overflow your coffee maker (oh man, I've done that at five in the morning). If it's too coarse then your coffee will taste weak and flavorless. Think about it like this. If you pour water over sand it takes the water longer to run through it and come out the other side than it would if you poured it over rocks. Maybe it would never come out. That's because the sand is so fine that there's fewer places for the water to go. With the rocks there is a lot more space in between each rock, and the water rushes through. A longer contact time allows for more extraction of flavor, while a shorter contact time extracts less.

Most grinds fall somewhere in this list (listed coarse to fine):

French Press – as coarse as you can get. It's the best way to brew. The grinds soak in the hot water, thus extracting more flavor. Additionally, since it's plunged with a screen it retains more of the flavorful oils, unlike a paper filter, which traps them. When using the appropriate water temperature and grind you should let it soak for about four minutes before plunging it.

Percolator – a very coarse grind is needed for a percolator. They aren't that common anymore but you can still find them around. This should be as coarse, or almost as coarse, as French Press.

Metal Cone or Paper Flat Filter – the most common setting. I never liked it when I would be asked to grind for a universal setting. If you don't know what setting you need and you have to have it ground now, then I would go with this one. This is a common scenario when it's a gift for someone. Starbucks stores use paper flat filters.

Paper Cone – it's fairly common. There is a difference between paper cone and paper flat so make sure you specify.

Espresso – this grind is what you need for brewing espresso at home – very fine, very fine indeed.

Turkish – super fine. It's basically a powder that borders on dust. It's used in preparing Turkish coffee, where the powder is boiled with sugar and served. It's not common in the U.S. but it's the norm in the Middle East.

Lastly, I should mention a couple things about grinding at home. As I said, it's best to grind on an as-needed basis. If you want to grind at home then I would suggest going with a burr grinder. It should be able to accommodate your specific needs. A blade grinder, on the other hand, isn't really a grinder. It slices and dices the beans until you tell it to stop. It's not nearly as accurate for obvious reasons.

The Clover – There's so much intrigue around the Clover that I figured I would address it here. The Clover is an altogether new brewing technology. In 2008 Starbucks purchased The Coffee Brewing Company, the manufacturer of the Clover, and began to test it in stores. There aren't many stores that have it. Stores that do, offer it as another method for brewing your drip coffee. It's not a machine that you can buy and take home. None of my stores had it but many around me did so I had opportunities to try it.

It uses Vacuum-Press technology to press coffee grinds through the hot water. It's similar to a French press in that way. Actually, it's kind of a super French press since it seems to produce more flavorful and vibrant coffee than an ordinary one. Stores that offer it also carry a lineup of specialty coffees. Many of these are rare and delicious. A cup of Clover coffee is a little more expensive than traditional drip coffee because of the select beans and the extra labor required to brew one. With that said, it's worth checking out if you get the opportunity.

3. Water

Water makes up the vast majority of volume in your coffee so you should pay attention to it. It's probably the fundamental that is most often neglected.

You want to use clean, processed water that still has some minerals in it. You don't want hard water because it will destroy your coffee maker or espresso machine. Soft or distilled water doesn't quite bring out the same flavors. Somewhere in the middle is ideal. Also, if your water has a funky taste to it, like that of chlorine, then you should treat it to get the best cup. Not only will that funky flavor transfer into your coffee (I've had some horrible cups) but it will hinder the coffee flavors.

You also should ensure that you're brewing at the right temperature. The water should be about 190-200°F to guarantee that it's doing all that it should be. Some people simply boil water (212°F at sea level). That's fine. If you're at some crazy elevation, say the top of Mt Everest (where water boils at 156°F), you may need to adjust accordingly.

4. Proportion

Finally, make sure that you're using the correct proportion of coffee to water. That proportion is two tablespoons of coffee to six ounces of water. Why isn't it 1:3? I don't know, maybe because no one drinks just three ounces of coffee.

Proportion is probably the most tampered with. I'm not going to say don't tamper with it but you shouldn't at first. To experience the full richness of the coffee you should stick with this ratio.

A lot of people say that they like their coffee strong so they add more scoops. Some say that it's too strong so they add more water. Before you add more scoops try a bolder coffee (it'll save you money too) and before you add more water try a milder coffee. When all else fails just make it however you like it. That's what really matters.

Cupping

Once you've brewed your coffee, you want to taste it. Cupping is the process of tasting coffee. Yes, there's an official process, just like wine tasting. If you want to participate in Starbucks coffee tastings, and slurp like a pro, then you'll need to follow these steps:

1. **Brewing**. It's imperative that you adhere to the four fundamentals previously listed. Brewing in a French press is really the best road to take for a lively cup. Your tasting will be pointless if you neglect the fundamentals.

2. **Smell the beans**. Before you grind them, take a few coffee beans in your hand, or on a spoon, and smell them. This will give you the fragrance of the coffee and whet your appetite.

3. **Cover**. Once you've poured your coffee, cover the cup with your hand. Not only will this preserve some heat while you gab about the coffee with others but it will trap the aroma.

4. **Breathe deep**. Next you want to take a deep breath and really absorb the aroma. You can do this in one of two ways. You can either lift your hand slightly and stick your nose in the cup or you can pull your hand away and stick your nose in as far as you can. What you do with your *schnauze* is your choice.

5. **Slurp**. You can't quietly sip away while you're tasting. You need to slurp, and slurp loudly. Slurping accomplishes two things. It helps prevent burning yourself and it helps spray the coffee over all of your tongue. The taste buds on different areas of your tongue detect different features. The tip will detect flavors and the back will detect bitterness.

Descriptors

After you've tasted coffee you need to describe it. The first thing you should know is that everyone's palate is different. What I think is bitter you might not find so bitter and when you taste a little cocoa I might not. This is true, of course, within a realm of reason. If I say it tastes like coffee you shouldn't be saying that it tastes like fruit punch. We'd have a real problem.

Another consideration to keep in mind is that coffee is a crop. That means it's affected by the weather, climate, events, and cultivating practices. The same coffee, but taken from different growing periods, may have a slightly different taste.

I recommend tasting multiple coffees during the same session, especially if you're new to the game. Contrasting different coffees is the best way to identify unique, and nuanced, characteristics.

When describing coffee, we want to do so within five categories: intensity, body/mouth feel, acidity, flavor, and aroma. Let's take a look at them.

1. Intensity. These are the most commonly used terms to describe coffee: mild, medium, bold, and extra bold. You use intensity descriptors to articulate the flavor. How intense is the flavor? Coffees with a powerful flavor are bold, a term that makes some coffee drinkers wary.

Starbucks currently roasts its coffees within three different categories that they label Blonde, Medium, and Dark. These categories aren't necessarily indicative of the coffee's intensity. Darkly roasted coffees tend to be bold but so do several medium roasted coffees. Sumatra is an extra bold coffee that is lighter than many of its extra bold counterparts.

2. Body. The body gets described in terms of light, medium, and full or heavy. The body is the "mouth feel". The best way to understand it is to compare it to milk. Nonfat milk has a light body compared to half and half, which has a full body.

3. Acidity. This is an important trait. It's often considered to be a desirable quality. African/Arabian coffees are known for it. To describe it I always think about the crispness of the flavors. If it's acidic the coffee will hit your tongue and be gone. It doesn't linger. It's bright and then dry. Generally, coffee becomes less acidic the longer it is roasted. You'll find that Starbucks' extra bold coffees have low acidity.

4. Flavor. The flavor of coffee can be rich – a particular flavor is distinct, complex – where many flavors make themselves known, or it can be balanced, where nothing in particular stands out. There's no doubt, though, that it's key when choosing a coffee.

Common flavor descriptors include caramel, chocolaty or cocoa, nutty, earthy, smoky, sweet, citrus, fruity, fragrant, spicy, bitter, syrupy, and more. It's important to note that these flavors tend to be subtle, like with wine. Spicy coffee isn't something you order in a Mexican restaurant. You might not even notice the spicy in your spicy coffee.

Also, pay close attention to the aroma because you'll need it to identify flavor.

5. Aroma. Aroma is key. It simply does it for a lot of people. They get a whiff of a pleasant aroma and they like the coffee even before tasting it. It aids in your ability to taste and you'll find yourself using some of the same descriptors that you use with flavor: caramel, cocoa, earthy, smoky, fruity, floral, and nutty.

Food Pairing

Sometimes customers will ask about food pairing – what food should be eaten with each coffee. The question usually comes up when having dinner guests, a holiday dinner, or serving dessert. The question really should be turned around to ask: What coffee should I have with my food? Usually, you pick a main course and prepare your meal around that. The whole point of pairing is to get the flavors in the food and the coffee to complement and amplify each other. Basically, you want them to make each other taste better. It's like choosing colors that won't clash when you're getting dressed. If you're ever in doubt then just go with a coffee that you really love. However, I can offer some advice.

Breakfast. Unless you're having a super hearty breakfast (I'm talking steak and potatoes) you'll want to keep it on the lighter side of the spectrum – mild or medium. The exception is if coffee is your breakfast. Then you might want/need something that is really hearty. You know who you are.

Lunch. It's hard to say. Lunch can include so many different meals, and maybe it's actually brunch. A middle of the road approach is usually best here. Medium Latin American and bold East African coffees are always good.

Dinner. The trend here says bold. That isn't necessarily the case. If you're eating a heavy dinner then maybe so but not if your dinner is on the lighter side – fish or poultry.

Dessert. If you're eating chocolate or cheesecake then the bold and extra bold coffees will serve you well. Think Gold Coast, Verona, French, and Italian.

Besides pairing around meals, you can pair around flavors. I've listed recommendations with each coffee later in the chapter.

Drip Coffee

When you visit Starbucks, and you're looking for a cup of drip coffee, know that there is a method to the brewing madness. Pike Place Roast, Decaf Pike Place Roast, a rotating bold coffee, and a rotating mild coffee are offered every day. The Pike Place is offered all day. The Decaf Pike Place and others may only be offered for a portion of the day depending on the store.

The list of rotating coffees changes. It also includes promotional coffees such as Guatemala Casi Cielo, Anniversary, Thanksgiving, and Christmas Blends. If these coffees are in season they'll be brewing at some point during their promotional period.

Let's say your favorite coffee is never brewed. Don't fret. If it isn't being offered then you can ask for a cup brewed in a French press at no extra charge. It'll take about seven minutes but it might be worth the wait.

Packaged Coffee

The coffee lineup carries a wide variety of mild, medium, bold, and extra bold coffees that hail from three regions: Latin America, Africa/Arabia, and Asia/Pacific. All coffees are in whole bean form. If you need it ground then the barista will grind it for you. Coffees generally come in one-pound bags (some promotional coffees are available in half-pound bags) but you can purchase any of them in quarter-pound increments; just ask. You can also ask to have blends made for you (i.e. half Caffè Verona and half Decaf Caffè Verona.)

Coffees also fall into one of three categories: 1) core – coffee that is available year round, 2) seasonal – coffee that makes an appearance once per year for a couple months, and 3) promotional – coffee that makes a time limited appearance but won't necessarily be back the following year. The line between seasonal and promotional coffees is somewhat blurred at times.

Core coffees encompass the larger part of the coffee offering and are segregated into three categories by roast: Blonde, Medium, and Dark. Blonde coffees tend to be quite mild and light bodied while Medium and Dark roast coffees are bolder with a heavier body.

Within the core offering there are currently seven decafs that are available all year for whole bean purchase: Willow Blend, House Blend, Pike Place, Verona, Espresso, Italian, and Sumatra. Historically, seven is a high number of decafs for Starbucks to be carrying so I would bet that a couple of those will be discontinued in the near future. Decaf coffees seldom make an appearance outside of the core lineup. Christmas Blend is one of the exceptions.

In addition to whole bean coffee Starbucks also offers an instant coffee – VIA Ready Brew. It's the same coffee that you get in the whole bean form but it's microground using a proprietary process. This means that it doesn't have any preservatives like other instant coffees do. It dissolves in water or milk, both hot and cold, and comes in little travel packets. The idea is to allow customers to have Starbucks coffee anywhere, even where there isn't a Starbucks.

Not every whole bean coffee is available in VIA. At launch it was Colombia, Italian, and Decaf Italian (not available in whole bean). Christmas Blend, French Roast, Iced Coffee, House Blend, Breakfast Blend, Veranda Blend, Colombia, and various flavored coffees (vanilla, mocha, caramel, and cinnamon spice) have since been added. I expect they will continue to add to the lineup.

The hype around the VIA launch was crazy. If you were a customer at that time then you probably remember it. I almost killed everyone in my store trying to sell it. Many customers loved it, some were skeptical of instant coffee, and others were turned off by all the hoopla. I'm not going to make some grand statement about it. Here's the bottom line: you can't replace drip or French pressed coffee, but for what it's meant to be it's a good product.

For those of you who own, or have access to, a Keurig Starbucks recently began carrying K-Cup packs for several of its coffees across the roast spectrum. As long as the Keurig continues to grow in popularity I imagine this product line will increase.

I often receive questions about Starbucks coffee purchasing practices. For the most part they operate under what is called Coffee and Farmer Equity Practices or C.A.F.E. These guidelines help protect both Starbucks and the coffee farmers. They ensure a high quality product for Starbucks and they require suppliers to show how much of the price was paid to farmers. C.A.F.E. Practices also requires compliance with a host of social and environmental conditions that help protect the farmers and the environment. About 84% of the more than 140 thousand tons of coffee that Starbucks purchases each year is purchased under C.A.F.E. Practices.

Starbucks is also the largest purchaser of Fair Trade Certified coffee. The Fair Trade organization, Fair Trade International, or FLO, is essentially a cooperative that allows workers to act in a manner resembling a union. It ensures a minimum price for coffee.

Latin American Coffees

Latin American coffees usually possess a mild or medium intensity. They offer a light to medium body, are often nutty, and contain cocoa notes.

Breakfast Blend. This is a milder coffee. At times it has been the mildest in the lineup. It has a light body with a hint of citrus. It's smooth and not overpowering. If you're new to Starbucks coffees then this might be a good place to start. House Blend, Pike Place, and other Latin American coffees will probably be your next steps up the coffee chain.

The company used to carry a decaf version but it was discontinued. If you're looking for something milder then try Veranda Blend or Willow Blend.

Pairs with: fruits and fruity pastries – blueberry, lemon, raspberry.

Colombia. It has a medium flavor intensity and a body that's a little heavier than Breakfast Blend. Its aroma is a little nutty. Its flavor has a nutty finish as well. This used to be a core coffee but has since become a seasonal offering.

Pairs with: nuts and pastries that contain nuts or have a nutty finish.

Guatemala Antigua. It's a medium coffee in the same category as Colombia and House Blend. Generally, it has a lingering chocolate flavor to it. It's subtle so pay attention or you'll miss it. Some describe it as being a little spicy too.

If you like it then check out Guatemala Casi Cielo in the winter.

Pairs with: It's easy to say chocolate because of the cocoa flavor in the coffee. It does pair well with that but also think about sweet, non-berry flavors that you like with chocolate such as caramel or hazelnut.

House & Decaf House Blends. Here's a coffee that you usually can't go wrong with. It's kind of the middle of the road. Since it's a blend of Latin American coffees you'll find it has cocoa and nutty notes along with a medium body and intensity.

If you enjoy it try either Pike Place Roast or a single origin Latin American coffee.

Pairs with: foods that contain chocolate or nuts, or food that pairs well with chocolate or nuts.

Veranda Blend. This is a light bodied coffee with a mild flavor intensity. Its flavors are very subtle. There's a nutty character to it and it has an ever so slightly cocoa undertone that you expect from Latin American coffees.

This is a good coffee for the new Starbucks customer. If you like it, then you might also like Willow Blend. If you're ready for a step up then try Breakfast Blend, House Blend or Pike Place Roast.

Pairs with: nutty and cocoa flavors; breakfast foods.

Africa/Arabia Coffees

African coffees are bold, acidic, and crisp. They often have a citrus undercurrent and floral aroma. For these reasons they also make good iced coffees.

Kenya is currently the only single origin African coffee offered by Starbucks but African/Arabian beans are used in several blends.

Kenya. This is one of my personal favorites. I love the citrus flavor that I always take away from it, or maybe I just like the picture of the elephant on the bag. Either way, I like it. It has a bold flavor and hefty body. I've heard it described in different ways but, like I said, I always take away that juicy citrus flavor which can be a little tart at times. Kenyan coffees are known for their acidity and that's certainly the case here. It jumps off your tongue.

Willow Blend contains some East African origins but without the same intensity. From time to time you'll find seasonal or promotional offerings that include East African coffee.

Pairs with: orange, lemon, lime, and grapefruit flavors.

Asia/Pacific Coffees

These coffees are bold and hearty. They're earthy, often spicy, and have low acidity. Their flavor tends to linger in your mouth.

Komodo Dragon Blend. The Dragon. This coffee is very similar to Sumatra. It doesn't get quite the same fanfare but it's still popular. It's bold, heavy bodied, spicy, and earthy. Its acidity is low.

If you like it, then you have to try Sumatra. Anniversary Blend is another similar coffee.

Pairs with: spices, cinnamon coffee cake, cinnamon scone. It also goes well with pumpkin.

Sumatra & Decaf Sumatra. Sumatra is the king-daddy-dog around Starbucks. Last I knew it was the best selling single-origin coffee in the company. It's very bold, heavy bodied, rich, and spicy. Its trademark feature is a deep earthy aroma that you really can't mistake. You'll find different herb and spice flavors within it.

If you're looking to try a Pacific coffee, then you should go for Sumatra. However, if you've had it and you're looking for something different, but similar, then Komodo Dragon and Anniversary Blends are good bets. If you're looking for other extra bold coffees, then Gold Coast, French and Italian are good. If you like Sumatra, perhaps the best recommendation I can make is Christmas Blend. It contains a significant amount of aged Sumatra. The downside, obviously, is that it's only available during the holidays.

The decaf version is decaffeinated through a purely natural process.

Pairs with: spices and herbs. You can't go wrong with cinnamon.

Anniversary Blend. This is another spicy option. It was originally brought into the lineup in 1996 to commemorate twenty-five years of Starbucks. It's been popular enough to stick around as a seasonal coffee during the fall. Usually, it's the promotional coffee offering right before Thanksgiving Blend.

It has your typical South Pacific features: spicy, earthy, full body, and bold.

Pairs with: spices such as cinnamon and nutmeg.

Multi-Region Blends

Christmas & Decaf Christmas Blend. It's the best. I don't know if it's my favorite (it's up there) but people love it. I've heard a hundred stories about those who stockpile it, trying to get through until the next holiday season. I can't exactly put my finger on what makes it so good. It has to be either the aged Sumatra (aged up to five years) or the way the Pacific and Latin American coffees play off of each other. In any event, it's excellent.

It varies every year but it's usually a little spicy (an Asia/Pacific characteristic) with some cocoa undertones (a Latin American characteristic). It just sets in your mouth so you can savor the flavors. That might be what sets it apart, not the flavors themselves. It's bold and usually has a medium to heavy body.

If you like it, try Sumatra, Komodo Dragon, or Anniversary Blend. It's also worth noting that Holiday Blend is Christmas Blend.

Pairs with: anything that is festive or spicy such as peppermint brownie, cranberry bliss bar, gingerbread, cinnamon coffee cake, and cinnamon scone. Gingerbread is probably the best.

Caffè Verona and Decaf Caffè Verona. Verona is quite possibly my favorite coffee. It's rich and sweet with a bold intensity and a medium body. It's hands down the best coffee to eat chocolate with. Verona is a blend of Yukon and Italian so if you're ever craving it, and your Starbucks is out of one-pound bags, just ask the barista to mix the two: 20% Italian, 80% Yukon.

If you like it, then try, of course, Yukon and Italian. They have the same characteristics.

Pairs with: chocolate and more chocolate.

Gold Coast Blend. This coffee is serious. It'll put hair on your chest. It's extra bold, full bodied, and has a myriad of flavors that bear witness to the several different coffees in its composition. I always take away a sweetness likened to Espresso Roast. It's a good coffee but its complexity isn't for the faint of heart.

As a side note, it's named for the posh Gold Coast neighborhood of Chicago that sits along Lake Michigan.

Yukon Blend and Espresso Roast are probably the closest in flavor and intensity.

Pairs with: caramel and cheesecake. The funny thing about cheesecake is that while I always recommend that as a good pairing for Gold Coast (it's simply perfect), Starbucks hardly ever sells it.

Iced Coffee Blend. This is the same iced coffee that's served in the store. Iced Coffee Blend is comprised of Latin American and East African coffees. East African coffees are great iced so that shouldn't be a surprise. Its intensity is middle of the road and it has a bit of a caramel sweetness to it. If you enjoy it iced try it hot as well.

If you are looking for another iced coffee I recommend Kenya. It's citrus notes are delicious when iced.

Pairs with: citrus flavors

Organic Yukon Blend. It has an image of being rugged and hearty. I mean, just look at the name, Yukon, and the bear on the package. However, it's probably lost some of its rugged reputation with the placing of *Organic* at the front of its name. Either way, it's a solid coffee. It's a bold blend of Pacific and Latin American coffees so it has a spicy bite to it. And if you're planning on taking an excursion into the wild anytime soon, this is what you should bring with you.

Except for lacking aged Sumatra, it's very similar to Christmas blend. If you like it you should also have Verona on your radar since Verona is composed of 80% Yukon.

Pairs with: cinnamon of course, since it has Pacific coffee in it. Chocolate is good too.

Pike Place Roast & Decaf Pike Place Roast. This is the "house" coffee if there is one. It was introduced in 2008. The idea behind it is to offer customers a consistent option at every store, every day. There are certainly many customers who aren't in love with it but that's because they generally prefer bolder coffee. Pike Place wasn't designed for that. What it does is open the door for non-Starbucks drinkers to try a coffee that won't completely overpower them and turn them off. It accomplishes both of these things.

It's a medium blend of mostly Latin American coffees. That makes it a little nutty with cocoa undertones. If you like it then you might enjoy House Blend as well.

Pairs with: chocolate and nuts.

Thanksgiving Blend. It only has a few years under its belt but it's proving itself. It's a full bodied and spicy coffee that's meant to be paired with traditional Thanksgiving foods – surprise! I think it accomplishes that.

Sumatra and Guatemala are good choices if you're looking to try similar coffees.

Pairs with: turkey, pumpkin pie, and sweet potatoes. You get the point - all of the Thanksgiving fixings.

Willow and Decaf Willow Blend. This is a bright, light bodied coffee with subtle flavors. It hails from Latin America and East Africa. It's a little acidic as you might imagine. Some of the flavors that you might find hidden in it are cocoa, nutty, and citrus. But like I said, it's pretty subtle. You might not taste any of them and find that it's simply a smooth and enjoyable cup of coffee.

Veranda is the most similar. If you're looking for the same flavors, but with greater intensity, then try Breakfast Blend, Guatemala Antigua, and Kenya.

Pairs with: fruit, nuts; breakfast foods.

Dark Roast Coffees

Espresso and Decaf Espresso Roast. This is the coffee of choice for espresso-based beverages. Starbucks uses it to make espresso and if you're looking for a coffee to use at home for espresso this is your best bet. However, its bold, full body is also good for drip coffee. There's a distinct caramel sweetness to it.

If you enjoy Espresso Roast as a drip coffee then you should try Italian and French Roasts. Italian Roast is also good when brewed as espresso.

Pairs with: caramel, of course.

French Roast. It's the darkest and boldest of Starbucks' offering. Actually, it's extra bold. Don't let the light body fool you because it's straight to the point. It'll smack you in the face. The most distinct aspect is its smokiness, both in aroma and flavor.

Italian Roast is a step below French but in the same extra bold ballpark.

Pairs with: chocolate of course. Doesn't it seem like that is the answer for everything? Rolls, bagels, croissants, and any kind of bread are all good. Break out the French baguettes!

Italian Roast and Decaf Italian Roast. Between French and Espresso Roasts, Italian Roast is a little smoky and quite sweet. It's extra bold with a medium body. Italian's features allow it to appeal to most coffee drinkers who enjoy bolder blends. The regular Italian Roast is also the only Fair Trade Certified coffee currently offered.

Espresso Roast and Caffè Verona are good coffees to try if you like this. If you want to go bolder then try French Roast.

Pairs with: spices, caramel, chocolate.

Chapter Three:

Tea

"You can never get a cup of tea large enough or a book long enough to suit me." – C.S. Lewis

"Remember the tea kettle – it is always up to its neck in hot water, yet it still sings!" – Unknown

O f course, water is the most popular beverage in the world. But after water it's tea that's consumed the most. How much tea does the world drink? Put it this way, tea consumption is equal to the consumption of all other produced beverages. That includes coffee, soda, alcohol, and chocolate. It's almost unbelievable, isn't it? The world is crazy about tea. And now that its health benefits are clear, Americans are getting crazy about it too.

Tea, like coffee, thrives in growing regions along the equator. The difference is that it grows in areas farther north and south. All tea comes from a plant called camellia sinensis. This includes black, green, white, and oolong teas – all teas that Starbucks has offered. The difference between each tea is in the processing. Tea is most commonly processed by wilting, fermenting, and oxidizing. Black tea is wilted and oxidized while green tea isn't.

Starbucks also offers a variety of herbal teas. However, herbal teas are not technically teas because they are not derived from the aforementioned tea plant. They consist, in large part, of flowers, herbs, roots, and berries. Therefore, you won't find any caffeine in them. Just to make it more complicated, you can purchase teas that mix herbal and traditional teas.

Health Benefits

Tea is all the rage for one reason: it's healthy. It's a super food really. It's high in flavonoids. And flavonoids are? You guessed it – antioxidants. Antioxidants neutralize free radicals, and free radicals are the agents that cause cancer in our bodies. Not only do antioxidants reduce the risk of cancer but they also reduce the risk of heart disease, arthritis, and more. So let the tea party begin (this is not a political statement)!

In addition to flavonoids, tea has more good news. Tea contains catechin, which is good for your teeth and gums. It also has caffeine (and you know how us Starbucks drinkers love our caffeine) and almost zero calories. This just keeps getting better. But remember, these benefits come from real teas, like green and black, not herbal beverages. While green and black teas are similar in their antioxidant content, green tea does have a little more because it endures less processing. It doesn't matter if it's hot or iced. Lastly, decaffeinated green and black teas will have fewer antioxidants as well. They're still worth it but they don't pack the same punch as their caffeinated counterparts.

Are there any negatives? Some studies have shown that tea can interfere with the body's ability to absorb non-heme iron, or iron gained from nonmeat sources. If you're a vegetarian with an iron deficiency then I wouldn't recommend drinking a lot of tea. With that said, don't listen to me – consult your doctor or nutritionist. They'll be able to give you much better advice.

Don't like tea? I used to hate it. So if you don't like it then there's still hope for you. Still, I knew it was good for me so I would force myself to drink it. Eventually I started to like it.

Packaging

There are really two ways to buy tea: loose full leaf or in a powder format that comes in a bag. For the same reasons that whole bean coffee stays fresh better than ground coffee, full leaf tea stays fresher than powdered tea. There's simply less air contact with larger pieces. Full leaf tea also has more flavor because it hasn't lost as much in processing. To steep it you need a pot with a strainer or filter, or you'll risk drinking your tea leaves.

On the other hand, powdered tea allows for a convenient steeping process because of the bag that it comes in. It has the same health benefits as full leaf.

Starbucks uses a combination of the two that's meant to give you the best of both worlds – full leaf tea in a bag. This gives you a sharper, more distinct flavor while allowing you to steep easily.

In both cases, if you want to keep your tea fresh then keep it in an airtight container. And don't freeze it.

Steeping

When steeping tea there are three things to be concerned with: water, tea, and time. You want the water to be about the same temperature as when you brew coffee – 190-200°F. You also want to use filtered water that won't hinder the flavors in the tea.

How much tea should you use? Unless you have a real appetite for something else you'll usually want to use just one tea bag. If you're using over sixteen ounces of water then you may need two, especially if you're not using full leaf.

How long you let your tea steep will obviously have a huge affect on the strength of the flavor. Some people only like to let their tea steep for a few seconds while others will never take the bag out. A good rule of thumb is to let black and herbal teas steep for five minutes and green teas for three to five minutes. If you're concerned about caffeine content then you can cut back on it by shortening the steeping time. If you want more caffeine then simply increase the steeping time.

Teas

Starbucks offers the Tazo brand of teas. Aside from Starbucks stores you can find Tazo teas in most supermarkets. In the supermarkets you might find a broader selection. You can also purchase Tazo Chai syrup in supermarkets if you're looking for that. A lot of customers ask about it. It's the same syrup that is used in Starbucks stores to make Chai Tea Lattes and Chai Crème Frappuccinos.

In case you're new to tea, you'll find that milk, lemon, and sugar are all nice additions. Starbucks doesn't offer lemons so if you really want one you'll have to bring your own or add it at home. And remember, it's not so fun to add lemon *and* milk.

Here's the lowdown on the teas that are routinely offered in Starbucks retail stores:

Black Teas

Awake – It's essentially an English Breakfast tea. If you're not familiar with tea that basically means it's a regular black tea. Oddly enough, American English Breakfast teas aren't the same as those served in England. True English Breakfast teas are heartier. These leaves are from India (second largest producer of tea behind China), Sri Lanka, and Kenya. You can order Awake iced as well.

Earl Grey – Another traditional tea. It consists of teas from India and Sri Lanka. It's a little citrusy and a little spicy. While there is no evidence to support it, the legend is that a Chinese mandarin gave British Prime Minister Earl Grey this tea as a gift for saving his son. The prime minister then promptly named the tea after himself. Go figure.

In addition to drinking, Earl Grey makes a good flavoring in sauces, chocolates, and baked goods.

Chai – This tea is a hodgepodge of teas from all around the world. It's a little spicy and has a kick to it. Interestingly, the word *chai* simply means *tea* in large parts of Asia. What we think of as chai is generally distinct to the Indian subcontinent. They serve a brand of chai tea that contains black tea leaves, spices, milk, and sugar. Sounds a lot like a Chai Tea Latte.

Green Teas

China Green Tips – Guess where this tea is from? If you go into a Starbucks and just ask for a green tea this is probably what you're going to get. It's your basic green tea and uses Mao Feng tea plants.

Zen – This might be the most popular green tea offered at Starbucks. Its tea leaves are from China. However, it's only partially tea. It also contains lemon grass and spearmint. Not surprisingly, it tastes a little lemony and minty. Zen is also available iced.

Orange Blossom – Believe it or not this is a green tea. It contains Chinese jasmine green tea, goji berries (better known as Chinese wolfberries), and tangerine peels. It's very floral, has a strong scent and, of course, has a citrus taste to it.

Herbal Teas

Calm – Calm consists primarily of chamomile and rose petals but also has lemongrass, spearmint, and sarsparilla. As you might expect, its taste is floral. It's intended to bring serenity. Starbucks says that it's like "sitting for 45 minutes in a mountain meadow on a sunny day with your shoes off." I don't' know about that but if you're having a particular stressful day then you may want to reach for one. Some customers say it works.

Passion – It has a distinct fruity taste. It contains hibiscus flowers, mango, papaya, and lemongrass. The fruity taste helps make this a good iced tea. It's available both hot and iced.

Refresh – This is the minty option. It contains peppermint, spearmint, and a little tarragon. It's good with chocolate and good if you have a cold. It'll open up your nose for sure. All of the ingredients of Refresh are grown in the United States.

Vanilla Rooibos – It's pronounced *roy-bus*. This tea contains rooibos (an African bush), Tahitian vanilla, peaches, apples and cinnamon. The taste ends up being rich and herbal. Rooibos is very popular in Africa, particularly southern Africa. It's high in antioxidants and is even used by Africans to treat asthma and allergies.

Other Options

Silver Tea – Little-known Silver Tea is another option. Actually, it's not tea at all. In fact, it's just hot water. Add a little honey or sugar and it's not bad. Honey is a very good addition, particularly if you're sick.

Tea Lattes – You can turn any tea into a tea latte. It includes your choice of tea, hot water, steamed milk, syrup if you wish to add it, and foam. Check out the *Beverages* section for more information.

Chapter Four:

Caffeine

"Sleep is a symptom of caffeine deprivation." – Unknown

"Caffeine isn't a drug, it's a vitamin." – Unknown

Caffeine is why many people come to Starbucks. They come to either get their day started or get that extra jolt that'll get them through the next few hours. There are so many questions and misnomers about caffeine. How much caffeine is in my drink? Does dark roast coffee have more caffeine? Is there a lot of caffeine in espresso? Does tea have caffeine? These are all questions that customers regularly ask. Let's shed some light on them.

The first thing to understand is that caffeine content is a variable quantity by nature. It's dependent on many factors including beans, roast, brewing, and steeping. Because of this we can only make educated guesses about caffeine content.

What is caffeine? Coffee and tea plants have caffeine, it is believed, as a defense mechanism against insects. Therefore the plant, especially a young plant, creates caffeine to ward off predators so that it can survive and grow. Does that make you feel more comfortable about drinking it?

With that said let's start with coffee. Robusta beans have considerably more caffeine than Arabica beans, and Starbucks uses Arabica beans. But don't be worried. There's still plenty of caffeine in your coffee.

Let's take a look at the difference between bold and mild roasted coffees. Some people believe that bold coffees have more caffeine and that they do a better job of waking them up in the morning. Some think there's significantly less caffeine in bold coffees because the caffeine gets roasted out. Caffeine doesn't get roasted out. Coffee beans expand as they are roasted. Darkly roasted coffees are roasted longer therefore they expand more than mildly roasted coffees. Since we measure coffee by volume dark roasted coffee will have less caffeine when brewed. The amount of caffeine in the beans doesn't change, just the size of the beans change. So, yes, bold coffees do contain less caffeine.

However, the difference is so small that it's negligible. If you're trying to gauge caffeine content, or you're concerned about your caffeine intake, I wouldn't base your decision on whether you get bold or mild. It's that insignificant. Caffeine content is usually measured in milligrams. On average, Starbucks drip coffee contains about twenty milligrams of caffeine per fluid ounce.

Espresso has far more caffeine, per ounce, than drip coffee. Starbucks espresso has around seventy-five milligrams. Don't let that fool you though. When people hear the word *espresso* they freak out and think that it must have tons of caffeine in it. The brewing method accounts for the discrepancy. Espresso is a much finer grind than traditional drip coffees made in a metal or paper cone filter. When you drip brew coffee, the water is flowing through semi-coarse grounds, and when you brew espresso it is flowing through fine grounds. It takes longer for the water to flow through finer grounds, thus the extraction time is longer and a much richer coffee is squeezed out of it. However, it's a little deceptive. That's because you might drink sixteen ounces of drip coffee but you don't drink sixteen ounces of espresso. At least most of us don't. In a sixteen-ounce espresso beverage you might have two or three ounces of espresso. Two ounces of espresso yields about 150 mg of caffeine. A sixteen-ounce black drip coffee yields about 320 mg. Milligram for milligram, espresso packs the strongest punch. If you compare drink to drink, which gives you a better idea of actual consumption, then drip coffee is where the real caffeine is at in the coffee world.

Tea generally has less caffeine than coffee but still a considerable amount. With that said, caffeine content is even more unpredictable. The plant varietal, age, growing season, growing region, water temperature, packaging, and steeping time, among other things, all factor in to caffeine content. Remember, only black and green teas contain caffeine. Herbal teas don't come from the camellia sinensis plant. They're generally flowers and herbs so they don't contain any caffeine.

With all of the variables that come with making a cup of tea it's almost impossible to give the precise level of caffeine for a single cup. One thing can be said for sure: the longer the steeping time, the more caffeine that will be extracted from the leaves. Generally, tea contains the following caffeine content:

Table 1: Caffeine Content of Tea

Beverage	mg / cup
Black Tea	50 - 90
Green Tea	35 - 70

You can control the caffeine content in your tea to a degree by adjusting the steeping time. As long as the bag is steeping it will continue to extract caffeine from the leaves. I know some customers who pull the teabag out as soon as they get their drink. If you leave the bag in the entire time you could consume more than ninety milligrams. If you don't take either of these drastic tea steeping methods then you can probably count on something in 35-90 mg range.

Besides tea, just how much caffeine is in your drink? Comparing the amount of milligrams per ounce gives you an idea of the beverage's caffeine potency. The table below compares the estimated per ounce caffeine content of some Starbucks coffee beverages with other popular beverages in our culture.

Table 2: Caffeine per Ounce

Beverage	mg/oz
Starbucks Espresso	75.0
Peet's Coffee Espresso	46.7
Starbucks Coffee	20.0
Starbucks VIA Ready Brew	16.9
Caribou Coffee Latte	15.0
Dunkin Donuts Coffee	13.2
Rockstar	10.0
Red Bull	9.5

Starbucks Grande Latte (16 oz)	9.4
McDonald's Coffee	9.1
McDonald's Latte	9.1
Hot Green Tea	7.0
Starbucks Tall Latte (12 oz)	6.3
Hot Black Tea	5.9
Mountain Dew	4.5
Hot Green Tea	3.1
Coca-Cola Classic	2.9
Starbucks Hot Chocolate	1.6
Starbucks Decaf Coffee	1.6
Instant Hot Chocolate	0.6

The next table shows the Starbucks beverages with the highest estimated caffeine content and their content when one and two additional shots of espresso are added. Remember the following sizes: short (8 oz), tall (12oz), grande (16 oz), hot venti (20 oz), iced venti (24oz), trenta (31 oz).

Table 3: Most Caffeinated Starbucks Beverages

	Beverage	**Recipe**	**+1 Shot**	**+2 Shots**
	Milligrams per Beverage			
1	Iced Trenta Coffee	420	495	570
2	Venti Coffee	400	475	550
3	Iced Venti Double Shot	375	450	525
4	Iced Venti Coffee	320	395	470
	Grande Coffee	320	395	470
6	Quad Espresso	300	375	450
	Venti Americano	300	375	450
8	Iced Grande Coffee	240	315	390

	Tall Coffee	240	315	390
10	Iced Venti Caramel Mac.	225	300	375
	Triple Espresso	225	300	375
	Grande Americano	225	300	375
	Iced Venti Latte / Mocha	225	300	375
14	Iced Tall Coffee	160	235	310
	Short Coffee	160	235	310
16	Doppio Espresso	150	-	-
	Venti Latte	150	225	300
	Grande Latte	150	225	300
	Tall Americano	150	225	300
	Venti Caramel Mac.	150	225	300
	Iced Venti Chai Tea Latte	150	225	300

Whoa, watch out for those black eyes! As you can see four of the top five drinks are drip coffee. With iced drinks you have to account for the ice. I've tried to do that as accurately as possible.

This fourth table shows an assortment of popular Starbucks beverages and their estimated caffeine content at various sizes.

Table 4: Caffeine Content of Popular Starbucks Beverages

Milligrams per Beverage

	Size (ounces)					
	8	12	16	20	24	31
					Iced	
Beverage	**S**	**T**	**G**	**V**	**V**	**T**
Americano	75	150	225	300	300	-
Black Eye	310	390	470	550	-	-
Cappuccino	75	75	150	150	-	-

Caramel Macchiato	75	75	150	150	225	-
Chai Tea Latte	50	75	100	125	150	-
Coffee	160	240	320	400	-	-
Decaf Coffee	15	20	25	30	-	-
Frappuccino	-	85	110	-	155	-
Green Tea Latte	30	55	80	110	-	-
Hot Chocolate	15	20	25	30	-	-
Iced Black Eye	-	310	390	-	470	570
Iced Coffee	-	160	240	-	320	420
Iced Red Eye	-	235	315	-	395	495
Latte	75	75	150	150	225	-
Mocha	75	75	150	150	225	-
Red Eye	235	315	395	475	-	-

A lot of Starbucks customers love their caffeine so these tables may be a welcome sight to you. If your drink doesn't have enough caffeine, or you feel that you need an extra kick once in awhile, then the solution is always to just add a shot of espresso, or two, or three. For those of you who are scared off by a lot of caffeine remember that you can always reduce the number of espresso shots if your beverage is espresso based. Just ask your barista how many shots are in your drink and then subtract accordingly. If you're drinking drip coffee, hot or iced, you can ask for extra ice, added water, or extra room. All of those modifications will cut down on the amount of caffeine.

Is there such a thing as a decaffeinated coffee? Is there any caffeine in decaf coffee? Tables 2 & 4 clearly show that there is caffeine in decaf coffee. So what gives? How can it be labeled *decaf*? The FDA requires that a coffee labeled *decaf* must have its caffeine level reduced by at least 97.5%. Arabica coffee beans are naturally about 98.65% caffeine free to begin with. That means about 1.35%, by weight, contains caffeine. The 1.35% that contains caffeine needs to be reduced by 97.5%. When that happens you are left with a coffee that is 3/100ths of 1% caffeinated. In other words, it's 99.97% caffeine free. So there is caffeine in decaf coffee – albeit a small amount.

This is why you'll see various claims about decaf coffee. Some advertising will claim that its product is 99.97% caffeine free, while others advertise 97.5% caffeine reduced. They're one and the same.

Water, in one form or another, removes the caffeine. It's usually removed by either a washing or steaming process. The removed caffeine is often sold to pharmaceutical companies for use in various medications.

If you want to reduce your caffeine intake, but still want some, try ordering your drink *half caff* and going from there. If you like a particular drink but you don't want the huge caffeine rush from it then you can probably get by with just ordering it decaf. If you absolutely cannot have caffeine in your diet then I would suggest purchasing a beverage that doesn't contain coffee or tea.

Chapter Five:

Modifying Your Beverage

"There is nothing wrong with change, if it is in the right direction."
– Winston Churchill

"If you don't like something, change it. If you can't change it, change your attitude." – Maya Angelou

A tall, espresso shot from the left spout of the left machine, let it sit for twenty seconds, nonfat milk to within one inch of the top of the cup, whole milk for the top inch, 170°F, no foam, latte.

A tall, chai syrup, extra hot, light caramel drizzle, whole milk foam, seven Splenda, steamed apple juice.

A venti, ten shot, no room, light ice, iced coffee.

Do these three drinks make any sense to you? Honestly, I have a hard time making sense out of them. That's how three different regular customers at my stores ordered their drinks. Granted, they are the extreme of the extreme, but that's what Starbucks customers do. They modify their drink until it's exactly what they like. Sometimes it gets crazy. The results range from the dull to the interesting and from the crazy to the downright horrifying.

Modifying your drink is the key to getting a beverage that you'll thoroughly enjoy. And, because most drinks are made from scratch as opposed to pressing a button, there's a lot that can be modified. This is one of the biggest reasons people are so wild about Starbucks. This is where the craziness starts to come in. It's where drinks that will make you run out of breath before you can finish saying them, come in. You know, the half caff, double, tall, one and a half pump, soy, extra hot, no foam, two equal, vanilla latte kind of drinks. Once you start to go down the road of modifying this is what happens. Every single drink on the menu can go down that road. No matter what you're drinking there are at least a dozen ways to modify it.

In this chapter we'll discuss the drink components that can be modified. Some modifications are commonplace but many aren't even listed on the menu. This will give you an idea of all the potential modifications that exist for drinks at Starbucks. I apologize in advance if your head starts to hurt. I've arranged a logical layout starting with basics, then with the order that modifications are listed on the cup, and finally odds and ends. If you're looking for a specific modification this will enable you to skip ahead and quickly find it. I've also boldfaced key words to aid in your search. The following chapter will show you how to apply these modifications to specific drinks.

Lastly, remember that modifications are just that: modifications. You should only speak them if you are deviating from the original recipe. Espresso drinks are presumed to be hot with regular espresso. If you would like a hot grande latte with regular espresso then you only need to order a *grande latte*. Don't over think it. It's complicated enough as it is.

Basics – The Cup

There are three categories of cups. They are paper cups, plastic cups, and ceramic/glass cups or mugs. Normally hot drinks are served in paper cups, iced drinks in plastic cups, and "for here" drinks in ceramic mugs.

There are four **paper cup sizes**:

- **Short – 8 oz**

- **Tall – 12 oz**

- **Grande – 16 oz**

- **Venti – 20 oz**

For all of you lifelong customers this is probably mundane, but for those new to Starbucks this might clear up a lot. Tall is small, grande is medium, venti is large, and short is the size that you've never heard of. We'll call it extra small.

Tall, grande, and venti are three ways to say large. *Tall* is, well, tall, or big. *Grande* is Italian for *large* and *venti* is Italian for *twenty*. I know, *venti* doesn't mean *large* but it is the large size. Weird.

All hot drinks are available in the short size. It's good if you don't want a lot to drink, are trying a new drink and don't want to pay for a larger size until you know you like it, or want to control your sugar, calorie, or caffeine intake. It's also the kids' size.

With the exception of shorts, hot drinks are usually served with a paper sleeve. Short cups are double cupped because the sleeves don't fit. If you don't like the sleeves you can have your drink double cupped. A lot of people like it that way. I used to do it myself but not anymore because it just isn't environmentally friendly.

Yep, I'm calling out all of you "double cuppers." Shame, shame. However, I suppose it's an acceptable excuse if the sleeves don't fit in your car's cup holder.

Iced drink sizes are as follows:

- **Tall – 12 oz**

- **Grande – 16 oz**

- **Venti – 24 oz**

- **Trenta – 31 oz**

Most hot drinks can be made iced. So if you have a favorite hot drink you can probably try it iced if you want. Many customers flip-flop hot and iced during summer and winter. However, if you're going to do this you should recognize a few things.

First, there is not a short size for iced drinks and there is not a trenta size for hot drinks. If you get a short hot drink, or an iced trenta drink, then you will need to change sizes when switching over.

Second, **trenta** (which means *thirty* in Italian) is only available for iced coffee and iced tea beverages.

Third, the iced venti size is four ounces larger than the hot venti size. Keep that in mind because it alters the drink's measurements.

Lastly, it may seem obvious, but there's ice in the iced drinks. A sixteen-ounce hot drink and a sixteen-ounce iced drink don't get the same amount of liquid in them because of the ice. An iced tall has the liquid volume of a hot short, and an iced grande is the equivalent of a hot tall, and so on.

Another option is ordering your drink "for here" in a porcelain cup. Some swear that their drink tastes better in porcelain compared to paper or plastic. If you don't notice a difference then at least you're saving some paper. If you want porcelain then you need to specify it. If you don't then you'll get hot drinks in paper and iced drinks in plastic.

Personally, I'm a fan of porcelain. It's just better. You don't drink out of plastic cups at home (well, maybe in college). Besides, you're saving that paper. It just feels a little more relaxing and "down home," if that makes any sense.

You can order all sizes in porcelain except for trenta. There are also tiny two-ounce cups for espresso shots called demitasse cups. *Demitasse* means *half cup*. It's a Euro thing I guess. I'd never be caught dead drinking out of one. I always get a venti porcelain cup no matter what size I order. I just can't get my fingers through the tiny little handle on the smaller sizes, you know?

Another alternative is having your drink made in **your own cup or mug**. Aside from saving the paper cup and plastic lid, you save ten cents. That's the discount offered for providing your own cup and you get a little taste of home out on the road.

Don't be embarrassed by your cup. It's your cup! I've seen some crazy ones and they're almost never washed. I don't know if I've ever seen the same mug twice. A lot of people have Starbucks mugs but not everyone. Many come in with Dunkin' Donuts cups, Green Mountain cups, traditional ceramic mugs, broken cups, some with crazy designs, and some that still have coffee or something else in it. People even come in with sixty-ounce cups and ask for them to be filled. That's serious business. Some come through the drive-thru without a lid on their cup and want it filled right to the top. These are usually the same people who are talking on their cell phone, have an iPod in the other ear, are eating with their other hand, and driving with their knee. Watch out. During wintertime some bring in mugs that are ice cold. You know that it's been in their car since the last time they had Starbucks. It's not uncommon to find frozen coffee in the bottom of it either. It might sound like I'm poking fun at these people (maybe I am a little) but it's actually quite funny because you can see yourself doing some of the same things.

Espresso

Espresso is one of the most common drink components. Lattes, mochas, cappuccinos, caramel macchiatos, and Americanos all have it. While it might sound straight forward at first there really is a lot that you can do with it.

When thinking about espresso keep in mind how much caffeine it has. This will play a large role. Remember, espresso has about 75 mg of caffeine per ounce. However, there is usually only one to four ounces of espresso in a typical espresso beverage.

You can add or subtract shots of espresso. You would do this for two reasons. First, if you want to increase your caffeine (I've got to have more!) you can add as many shots as you wish. Likewise if you want to decrease your caffeine intake you can order fewer.

Secondly, you might adjust the number of espresso shots to alter the coffee flavor intensity. If the coffee flavor is too much for you then you may want to consider fewer shots. You can even order just 1/4, or 1/2 of a shot. Conversely, you can add shots to intensify the coffee flavor. If you want more coffee flavor without adding caffeine just order the additional shots decaf.

If you want to sound like you know what you're talking about then order one shot as a *solo*, two shots as a *double* (When ordering just espresso order a *doppio*), three shots as a *triple*, and four shots as a *quad*. Check with your barista to see how many shots your drink gets. You might want a double but your drink may already be a double.

Of course you can get your latte, or any other espresso drink, decaffeinated. But did you know that you can also order it partially decaffeinated? Adjusting the caffeine level is the most basic way of modifying espresso. You can order it 1/4, 1/2, or 3/4 decaf if you want some caffeine. Ask your barista how many shots (1 shot = 1 ounce) are in your drink. If there are three it's easy to make your drink 1/3 or 2/3 decaf. You can break down the caffeine percentage anyway that you can imagine.

A lot of customers worry about accidentally getting a caffeinated drink when they ordered decaf. That's a legitimate concern because regardless of who is making drinks mistakes will happen from time to time. Though it may not always appear it, because baristas can rattle off drinks while seemingly unconscious, they are human.

There's a slight taste difference between caffeinated and decaffeinated espresso. You can tell the difference. I drink decaf on a daily basis. When I get my usual drink and it's made with caffeine I know as soon as I take the first sip. If you drink the same espresso beverage every day, regular or decaf, and you're given the other you should be able to tell fairly easily.

There are other modifications to make, in addition to those listed above, if you're ordering just espresso. You can also order espresso shots **long** or **ristretto**. A long shot is brewed with more water than a traditional espresso shot. It ends up having about two to three times more volume. A long shot is weaker and more bitter.

The extra water extracts more from the grinds. The longer the shot then the weaker and more bitter it will taste.

The opposite holds true for a ristretto shot of espresso. Less water is passed through the grinds therefore the resulting espresso shot is smaller, stronger, richer, and less bitter. It's a lot like a traditional shot of espresso but with its characteristics more pronounced.

You can also add milk foam or whipped cream. Adding foam creates an **espresso macchiato** and adding whip makes an **espresso con panna**. Both are common.

Lastly, you can order a drink *affogato*. Affogato means *drowned*. At Starbucks it really means pouring a shot of espresso on top of a beverage. It's usually ordered in Frappuccinos. The Frappuccino is made and then a shot of espresso is poured, or laid, on top. In Frappuccinos an affogato shot lays, or sits, on top nicely but in hot drinks it mixes in quickly.

"Domo affogato Mr. Roboto . . . domo . . . domo." Whenever someone orders affogato that's all I can think of. Now that song will be stuck in your head for a couple days. You're welcome.

Flavors

Flavor is probably the most modified item after espresso and milk. You can flavor your drink with a syrup if you wish. However, keep in mind that the flavored syrups contain sugar. Vanilla and hazelnut are common but you can also get caramel, cinnamon dolce (pronounced *dōl-chay*), peppermint, raspberry, toffee nut, chocolate (mocha), white chocolate (white mocha), and chai syrups. During their respective seasons pumpkin spice, caramel brulée and gingerbread are offered as well. All three are popular, especially pumpkin spice. There are various other flavors temporarily available as promotions from time to time. Just ask to find out what they are. There are also **sugar-free flavors** that include caramel, cinnamon dolce, hazelnut, and vanilla. Other sugar-free flavors have been available from time to time, especially mocha.

Flavors at Starbucks usually come in the form of syrups and sometimes powders. Many coffee shops will offer coffee that has flavor roasted into it. That's never the case here.

Many times I've heard a customer say, "I really like vanilla lattes but they're a little too sweet." Or maybe they'll comment about how they're trying to cut down on the amount of sugar or calories in their diet. The sugar-free syrups do taste a little different than their sugar-filled counterparts. So it's not uncommon to want a lesser amount of sugar but the same sugar taste. To do this you modify the amount of syrup in your drink.

I won't get into the specific amount of pumps in each drink. I will say that plenty of people order drinks with only half the amount and plenty get additional. You can even ask for half of a pump if you want. This is a good way to control the sweetness of your drink as well as the calorie count. If you want to know how many calories are in a pump of syrup then just ask for the nutritional information on the beverage. You might be able to find it at the condiment bar too.

Another thing you can do with flavors is mix them. Half vanilla and half hazelnut is a popular one. That's referred to as **French vanilla**. Caramel, peppermint, and raspberry all pair well with chocolate, or mocha. Then again, every flavor pairs well with chocolate.

There's also a flavorless syrup, Classic, that you can sweeten your drink with. It mixes well and gets the same job done as white sugar. Some refer to it as simple syrup.

Milk

Milk is a prime component of many drinks. Lattes, cappuccinos, macchiatos, hot chocolates, and mochas all need it. It's crucial that milk is aerated just right, is the right temperature and has the right amount of foam. It also needs to be served within a reasonable amount of time. Because these are handcrafted beverages made to order it depends, to a degree, on how skilled your barista is. The espresso machines used at Starbucks are incredible but they don't steam perfect milk on their own. Generally, it's a non-issue. However, if you're particular about your foam then pay attention.

Varieties – The available dairy options are: whole, nonfat, 2%, 1% (by mixing 2% and nonfat), half and half (breve), heavy cream, soy, and eggnog (available in November and December). You might be able to get organic milk but at the time of this writing it was discontinued in most markets.

If you don't specify what kind of milk you want then you'll be getting the default. In espresso drinks the default is 2%. The exception is ordering your drink *skinny*. That'll get you nonfat milk but we'll get more into that later on. Frappuccinos default to whole milk and Light Frappuccinos default to nonfat milk.

The soy is good. It appears to be specially formulated so it won't curdle when mixed with coffee. A drink made with breve is a risky proposition. As you can imagine there's some serious fat in that. To each their own, right? I have to admit that I've been known to drink a short hot chocolate made with breve every now and then. Heavy cream is hardly ever used in a drink. I think I've seen it once or twice. The option is available if you can find a reason to use it.

Aside from choosing one of these milks you can always mix two of them in your drink. No matter how odd the combination there is someone doing it somewhere. There are customers who order half soy and half nonfat. That isn't uncommon.

Foam – If you want foam then you probably want it to be rich and creamy. Improperly aerated milk usually creates very little foam or none at all. If it's aerated too much it creates large bubbles. You end up with foam that's like soap suds and then quickly disappears.

One of the most popular ways to modify foam is to order extra. If you're a foam nut then you're probably doing so already. Try to be specific about what extra is. Specifying in inches is good. You can also dial up the dollops. Drinks normally receive about one dollop, or spoonful. Two or three is a hefty amount. Anymore than that and you're getting into cappuccino territory.

Foam is especially crucial when ordering a cappuccino. You get cappuccinos because you like foam. When made to the common standard they're essentially half milk and half foam. You can order them **wet**, with less foam and more milk, or **dry**, with more foam and less milk.

Making a dry cappuccino can be tricky. The milk has to be aerated longer to obtain a depth of creamy foam. If not you'll end up with either too little foam or the aforementioned soap suds. It's especially tricky to create a lot of quality foam with soy or nonfat milk. Remember, fat makes good foam so breve, whole milk, and even 2% are your best bets.

Many customers like their cappuccino "bone dry," or almost all foam. If you want to modify the foam in your cappuccino you should be as specific as possible. *Dry* and *wet* are subjective terms. Using specific amounts such as 70% or 3/4 is the best way to ensure that you get what you want.

Another way of modifying foam is to order one kind of milk and another kind of foam. Why would you do that? Because you love foam, of course. We said that the higher the fat content, the creamier the foam will be. If you order a drink made with nonfat milk, but whole milk foam, then you'll keep calories down and still allow for top-notch creaminess.

Maybe you don't even like foam. You can order your drink without it. Many do. Drinks that are made with milk but don't get whip on top are usually made with foam automatically. So if you don't want either then you'll want to specify that. Negating foam can be a tricky thing to do sometimes. Bubbles may occur in the beverage simply from it being mixed. Your drink may appear to have foam at times but in actuality it doesn't. It just needs some time to settle.

Even if you don't want foam you should want the barista to steam really great foam for your beverage. Doing so will aerate the milk properly. If the milk isn't aerated properly then it'll taste flat.

Temperature

You can control the temperature of your drink, some more than others. With many drinks you can specify a specific temperature but with others you can only cool it down or warm it up.

Steaming to a specific temperature is a modification reserved for milk and sometimes juice. Bar drinks are normally around 155°F. If you order a kids drink then it'll be around 130 – 140°F. That's not very hot, just warm. Order your drink extra hot and it'll be around 170°F. Extra, extra hot will get you a drink around 180°F. While you can certainly think of plausible reasons for ordering a drink that is hotter than 180°F, for the most part, I don't recommend it. Too far beyond that will generally start scalding the milk, or at least affect the quality of the beverage. At about 200°F it starts to explode out of the pitcher. I don't think I've ever made a drink hotter than that (mainly because I don't like 200°F milk exploding on me), and only then when I wasn't paying attention. As always, remember that terms like *extra hot* are subjective and won't always yield consistent results.

If *extra hot* is good enough for you, then great. If you want your drink to be exactly the same temperature every time then you should order a specific temperature. Ask the barista what temperature your beverage is normally made at (probably around 155 degrees, give or take three or four degrees) and modify from there. By being specific and ordering a "165°F latte" instead of an "extra hot latte" you're ensuring that your beverage will be made at the same temperature every time, no matter who makes it. It's a crucial factor. Getting a drink at the wrong temperature can ruin your experience. You want a Goldilocks temperature that's juuust right.

You can't order a specific temperature for a drink that isn't steamed. These include coffee, tea, Americanos, Frappuccinos, and any iced beverages.

Coffee, tea, and Americanos use 190°F water. If you want to make them cooler your best bet is to add ice or cold water. You can't make them hotter.

Tea lattes, including chai tea lattes, are made with hot water and steamed milk. When you ask to alter the temperature of these you're only altering the milk portion. The water is still 190°F.

I suppose you can make iced and frozen drinks warmer or colder by adjusting the amount of ice or removing it altogether. I guess an iced latte without ice is actually an extra hot iced latte.

Sugar

Adding sugar to your beverage is another popular way to modify. Just ask and the barista will add white sugar, raw sugar, Equal, Splenda, or Sweet and Low. It's best to specify the number of packets to ensure consistency. You can always add it yourself at the condiment bar as well. You can also bring your own sugar. Some customers do that. Maybe you like Stevia or brown sugar. Starbucks doesn't carry those.

Also, if you're planning on adding sugar keep in mind that there's sugar in the flavored syrups already. Let's say you order a vanilla latte. There's sugar in the vanilla flavoring so you may not want to sweeten it with four packets of Splenda right away.

Whipped Cream

Making whipped cream is a daily task at Starbucks, and one of the first tasks that new baristas learn. Made incorrectly and the whip will explode everywhere – on the walls, the baristas, the countertops, everywhere. I've even walked into the store to find whip on the ceiling. The key is to ensure that the whipped cream container has the required gasket. Many times new baristas will forget it. Sometimes it's intentionally left out by the trainer – a hazing of sorts for new partners. Oh, the joys of the job.

Everyone loves whip, or at least they should. In case you don't know, it's made with vanilla syrup and heavy cream. Mochas, white mochas, hot chocolates, cinnamon dolce lattes, almost all Frappuccinos and various promotional beverages already include it. You don't have to ask for it on those. Otherwise, if you want it then you'll have to ask.

Many customers seem to be quite passionate about their whip. I don't know what it is but there's just something fun about whip that draws people in. Many will order their drink nonfat to cut back on calories so they won't feel as guilty adding it. Other customers like to add whip when it's Friday, or the weekend, or to let loose and indulge a little. Extra whip is a big deal. Some even order a tall or grande beverage inside a venti cup to create extra space for it. Now that's some serious celebrating!

Making whip from scratch also makes it easy to experiment. If you have some extra time you can always ask your barista to whip up some peppermint or chocolate whip if you'd like to try it. Those are pretty tasty. It's uncommon for a customer to request those but it's something that you might like to try. Besides, the baristas will have fun sampling the rest.

Another tasty little treat to try is a cup filled with whipped cream and chocolate or caramel drizzle on top of it. It's good but make sure you ask for a spoon.

If the drink that you're ordering comes with whip you can always specify that you don't want it. Remember, if your drink is hot then you may automatically get foam as a substitute.

Lastly, dogs love whip too! Many customers get a short cup with whip for their furry companions.

Drizzle

Sauce, or drizzle, is another good modifier. For those who have a sweet tooth you can have chocolate or caramel sauce drizzled on top of your beverage. Both flavors are popular and quite tasty.

Caramel drizzle already comes on a Caramel Macchiato, Caramel

Apple Spice, Salted Caramel Hot Chocolate, and Caramel Frappuccino. Having it on a caramel mocha is good too. After espresso it's probably the ingredient where extra is most often ordered.

Chocolate drizzle is included in hot chocolate, Double Chocolaty Chip Frappuccino, and Java Chip Frappuccino. The sauce is the same as the chocolate, or mocha, syrup used in mochas and hot chocolates. It's just used in a different capacity.

Drizzle doesn't have to be applied to the top of the beverage. It's also popular in the bottom and along the insides of the cup.

Occasionally there are promotional beverages that use these two drizzles or offer a new one altogether.

Powders

There are three powders that are used in select beverages and can be applied to others as well. They include: protein and fiber, vanilla bean, and green tea matcha.

We'll start with **protein and fiber powder** because it's one of my personal favorites. It's simply whey protein and fiber. Certainly it's a healthy addition if you can find a way to take advantage of it. The only mainstay beverages that use it are the smoothies. That's usually where it comes into play and oftentimes customers specify more or less of it. You can add a scoop or two of it to other drinks. It's a great addition in milk-based beverages such as lattes and mochas.

The powder slightly changes the taste and the texture. The best way I can describe the taste is that it's ever so slightly sweeter than a plain latte. The texture is a little creamier than usual, thus making the drink lighter to the touch. Any flavors that work well in lattes will work well with the protein and fiber powder. I find that people are usually turned off when I mention it but are pleasantly surprised when they try one.

To make it, the powder needs to be steamed into the milk. That's one of the trickiest things to do. It's right up there with bone-dry cappuccinos. Not many baristas are adept at constructing this because there aren't any hot drinks on the menu that incorporate it.

If you decide to try one and your barista doesn't know how to make it you can tell them how. Active steaming really is the key. If it's stirred in you'll have a drink full of protein chunks. I don't know about you but, like most people, I like to drink my lattes, not chew them. Active steaming means the barista needs to aerate the milk the entire time it's steaming. Usually milk will be aerated for several seconds and then left to finish on its own while the barista does something else. That can't happen when steaming protein powder because it'll result in the same chunky mess as stirring it. You can tell as soon as you pick one up if it's been made correctly. If it feels heavy like a latte then it's definitely wrong. And when it's wrong, it's wrong. You really can't even drink it. It's disgusting. However, if it's correct, and feels lighter like a cappuccino, then it's an excellent drink and a good way to get extra protein and fiber into your diet. Veteran partners should be able to make one for you because it was a promotional drink several years ago.

Vanilla bean powder is only used regularly in Vanilla Bean and Café Vanilla Frappuccinos. It's a great addition in Frappuccinos because it mixes in so well. It can be used in hot drinks. I know customers that prefer to have their vanilla latte made with vanilla bean powder instead of vanilla syrup. I've never tried it but they feel they're onto something.

Then there is **green tea matcha powder**. It's only a regular ingredient in Green Tea Latte and Green Tea Frappuccino. When included in a hot beverage it's steamed into the milk and creates a creamier texture. It steams in much easier than the protein powder. When included in a cold drink it's either stirred or blended in. There's not a lot of craziness around matcha powder but you might be able to think of something creative to do with it if you like green tea.

Room

You can ask for extra room in your drink. Without specifying you should get about a quarter-inch of room. Room is usually requested in drip coffee or tea so dairy can be added at the condiment bar. If you're worried about your drink spilling then you can ask for some "walking room."

Again, *room* and *extra room* are subjective terms. You should always be as specific as possible. Ask for "an inch" or "one and a half inches." If you're getting a short, tall, or grande size then you can ask for it in a larger cup if you want extra, extra room or don't want to lose any of your beverage to room.

Skinny

Skinny is a term often used to define a nonfat drink. At Starbucks it connotes drinks that contain nonfat milk, sugar free syrup, and lack whip. Only four drinks can be truly skinny. Those are Skinny Vanilla Latte, Skinny Hazelnut Latte, Skinny Caramel Latte, and Skinny Cinnamon Dolce Latte. That's because those are the only flavors offered in a sugar free form. The drinks are completely sugar free because there is still some sugar in the milk but the flavoring is sugar free. Keep that in mind.

Skinnies are quite popular, especially vanilla. Get yours with decaf espresso and you have a "no fun latte." That is no fat, no sugar, no whip, and no caffeine. What's the point again?

The menu does offer a Skinny Caramel Macchiato but it's not completely sugar-free. It contains nonfat milk and sugar-free vanilla syrup but the caramel drizzle is not sugar-free. It's also worth noting that Skinny Mochas have been available from time to time.

If you just want a nonfat latte without flavoring then you should order just that: a nonfat latte. Truth be told, if you want to order a *nonfat latte* but you order a *skinny latte* you could cause some confusion. Stop messing with the baristas!

Ice

Most hot drinks make excellent iced drinks. Coffee, tea, lattes, caramel macchiatos, mochas, Americanos, chai tea lattes, and espressos can all be made iced. Actually, they're all very popular iced. This is especially true in warm markets and during the summertime, as you can imagine. Although, plenty of people always like their drink iced, even when it's -10°F outside. Just as plenty of people always like their drink 180°F even if it is 105°F outside. So don't worry, you're not weird.

Cappuccinos and macchiatos iced? I don't know about that. I saw maybe five per year. The baristas will make them if you ask (there are recipes for them) but I'm not about to recommend them. If you think that you want an iced cappuccino you probably want an iced latte. An iced cappuccino has foam on top of the ice. The foam dissipates quite quickly. As I've said before, to each their own, but you're getting hot foam on ice so you do the math. Besides, you're going to turn heads ordering this one. "We've got a crazy here!"

Extra ice, *light ice*, and *no ice* are all potential modifications. Are you wondering how an iced drink can have no ice? Well, it can still be made with cold liquids. It just doesn't get ice.

Extra ice can be used to cool down hot drinks. Hot Americanos are often ordered with ice cubes to ready them for immediate consumption. The same goes for coffee and tea.

If you order light ice then you'll probably get a little more of the other ingredients such as milk and water (depending on what your drink is made with but not necessarily so) but it won't stay cold for as long either. I don't have a recommendation here. You can weigh your ice priorities.

You might not believe this but it's not uncommon for someone to order a specific number of ice cubes. Some people like five ice cubes, some like only two. Maybe that's in their iced drink or maybe it's in their hot drink. Those are both heady options.

Other Modifications

For the sake of space I have listed all other ingredients and modifications here.

Upside down. This is commonly applied to Caramel Macchiatos but sometimes to other drinks. It refers to constructing the beverage backwards, or upside down. Caramel Macchiatos first get vanilla, then milk, foam, espresso, and caramel sauce. When making it upside down the caramel sauce goes in first. Next is espresso. This mixes the drink a little better. It's designed to be layered, not mixed. If you would prefer it mixed then this will make that happen. Ordering your Caramel Macchiato upside down will construct it like a traditional latte but with caramel sauce in the bottom of the cup.

Chocolate Curls. These are usually available around the holiday season and throughout the winter. They're intended to go on Peppermint Mochas, Peppermint Hot Chocolates, and Peppermint Mocha Frappuccinos. They're certainly good for these drinks. However, they're a nice topping for any drink if you want to add some chocolate.

There are also a variety of **powdered toppings** to sprinkle on your drink. Vanilla, cinnamon, nutmeg, vanilla bean, cinnamon dolce (basically a sweet cinnamon), chocolate and, if the season is right, pumpkin spice are all available flavors. It's a good way to add a subtle something extra to your drink.

Shaken. The only drinks that are regularly shaken are iced teas and the Starbucks Double Shot. Iced coffees used to be shaken. Shaking only works for iced drinks. If you want your iced drink a little foamy, or you want to make sure that it gets mixed up extra well, then try ordering it shaken.

Lemonade. It is available. Usually it's only ordered in iced tea. You can vary the amount added to your iced tea or get it on its own. For the record, Starbucks doesn't carry lemons. If all you want is an iced tea with a lemon slice then you need to slice a lemon. A good alternative is a splash of lemonade.

Apple Juice. It's available year 'round in the Caramel Apple Spice. You can also order it on its own, hot or cold. There isn't a lot you can do with it but some customers like steamed apple juice with chai tea syrup. That makes an Apple Chai.

Butter. You're probably wondering why butter is listed as a modification for drinks. I'm still trying to figure out why I listed it myself. Well, the truth is I've never seen anyone put butter in their drink. However, I did have a manager tell me that he had a regular customer who ordered two butter patties melted into his latte. I'm not listing this because I'm recommending it. I'm listing it because I think it's crazy and you might find it funny. I dare you to try it.

Bananas. No, I'm not going to recommend that you slice a banana into your latte. Bananas are a regular ingredient in smoothies. You can always have it taken out or have extra banana added in. Frappuccinos are good drinks to add bananas to. The chocolate flavored Frappuccinos would all pair well with some amount (probably a half or a whole) of banana added.

If you want a slice of banana into your latte then go ahead. After the butter patties nothing surprises me.

Chocolate Chips. Chocolate chips are only an ingredient in two drinks: Java Chip Frappuccino and Double Chocolaty Chip Frappuccino. However, if you want to add them into any other Frappuccinos then you are certainly welcome to. I think they pair well in a lot of them.

Conclusion

Ultimately any component can go anywhere. That's dependent on your preferences. Hopefully this section will get your creative juices flowing so you can try some new beverages, or new takes on your favorite beverage. So start experimenting!

Chapter Six:

Beverages

"I didn't miss the cappuccino, I missed the idea of cappuccino."
– Martha Stewart

This is probably the part of the book that you've been waiting for. You can learn more about each drink, especially your drink, and the popular ways to modify them.

Each drink profile answers the following questions:

What's in the drink?

What does the drink taste like?

Who would like the drink?

How can the drink be modified?

What are some recommendations?

Hopefully this section will tell you everything you want to know about ordering and enjoying Starbucks beverages.

Notes for Espresso and Non-Frappuccino Based Beverages

The following modifications are available when discussing espresso based and non-Frappuccino beverages:

Cup – short (hot only), tall, grande, venti (cold is 4 oz. larger than hot), trenta (iced coffee and tea only); "for here" porcelain is available; double cup.

Espresso – decaf; 1/2, ¼, ¾, 1/3, and 2/3 decaf; ristretto, long; add and subtract shots.

Syrup – caramel, chai, chocolate (mocha), cinnamon dolce, Classic (flavorless liquid sugar), hazelnut, peppermint, pumpkin spice (seasonal), raspberry, toffee nut, vanilla, white chocolate (white mocha), sugar free caramel, sugar free cinnamon dolce, sugar free hazelnut, sugar free vanilla, and current promotional syrups.

Milk – whole, 2%, 1%, nonfat, soy, breve (half and half), heavy cream, organic (potentially in some markets), eggnog (seasonal).

Sugar – white sugar, raw sugar, Equal, Splenda, Sweet & Low.

Temperature – extra hot, kids temp, specific temp.

Whipped Cream – extra, light, none.

Foam – extra, light, none, dry, wet.

Powders – green tea matcha, protein and fiber, vanilla bean.

Spice Toppings – chocolate, cinnamon, cinnamon dolce, nutmet, pumpkin spice, vanilla.

Other – room, upside down, chocolate chips, honey.

Notes for Frappuccino Beverages

Frappuccino beverages fall into three categories:

Coffee Frappuccinos – centered around coffee, whole milk, and base syrup.

Coffee Light Frappuccinos – centered around coffee, non-fat milk, and light base syrup.

Crème Frappuccinos – centered around whole milk and crème base syrup; doesn't contain coffee.

- Technically, Crème Frappuccinos don't have a light version. However, you can make them somewhat light by substituting nonfat milk and leaving out the whip.

- The coffee used in Frappuccinos is called Frappuccino Roast. There isn't a decaf Frappuccino Roast so if you order a decaf Frappuccino then decaf espresso is substituted.

- Technically, coffee Frappuccinos are called "Coffee Frappuccino Blended Coffee." Therefore a Java Chip Frappuccino is technically called a Java Chip Frappuccino Blended Coffee. No one really uses that terminology because it tends to be long and confusing. Crème Frappuccinos are technically called "Crème Frappuccino Blended Crème."

- Frappuccinos are available all year.

The following Frappuccino modifications are always in play:

Cup – tall, grande, and venti cups.

Lids – flat and dome lids (served on drinks that contain whip).

Coffee – Frappuccino Roast - more, less, or none.

Espresso – add shots; affogato; decaf.

Milk – whole, 2%, 1%, nonfat, soy, half and half, heavy cream, organic (if available), eggnog (seasonal).

Whipped Cream – extra, less, none.

Ice – more, less, none; smoothie, tall, grande, and venti scoop sizes.

Sweetness – adjust base syrup amount.

Syrup – caramel, chai, chocolate (mocha), cinnamon dolce, Classic (flavorless liquid sugar), hazelnut, peppermint, pumpkin spice (seasonal), raspberry, toffee nut, vanilla, white chocolate (white mocha), sugar free caramel, sugar free cinnamon dolce, sugar free hazelnut, sugar free vanilla, and current promotional syrups.

Powders – green tea matcha, protein and fiber, vanilla bean.

Spice Toppings – chocolate, cinnamon, cinnamon dolce, nutmet, pumpkin spice, vanilla.

Other Liquids / Mixes – strawberry sauce, orange mango sauce, lemonade, apple juice.

Other – bananas, chocolate chips, double blend.

Americano

Ingredients: *espresso, hot water*

Caffè Americanos, or *Americanos*, are made with espresso and hot water. You can order them iced as well. In that case ice and cold water replace the hot water. The name comes from American soldiers who were stationed in Europe in the early part of the twentieth century. The soldiers didn't like straight espresso because they felt it was too strong. They weakened it by adding water.

It's just watered-down espresso so it tastes a lot like a regular cup of coffee. If you like coffee then you'll probably like Americanos. If you're in Starbucks and for some reason brewed coffee is unavailable, a possible anomaly, then try an Americano as a substitute. You might be pleasantly surprised.

Usually, it's treated like a cup of coffee. Customers commonly add dairy, sugar, and extra espresso to it. Adding syrup to an Americano isn't very common but if you do it's not all that weird either. Vanilla, hazelnut, and Classic syrup are the most popular syrups.

A hot Americano is normally served at about 190°F. If you're looking to add milk but would like to keep the drink as hot as possible then ask the barista for a little steamed milk instead of opting for the cold milk at the condiment bar. Adding some foam in the process is also nice. It's not possible to make an Americano extra hot because it's made with hot water, not steamed milk. If you would like to cool it down you can add ice or cold water.

If you like Americanos, but they're not quite strong enough, you can order a large size in a smaller cup, like a venti size in a grande cup. Don't worry, it won't spill all over the place. It'll give you a stronger tasting drink without adding more shots to it because all you're doing is adding less water. If you like having a larger cup then ask for it with *extra room* or *half full*.

Common Variants – iced Americano.

Common Modifications – added dairy or soy, steamed dairy or soy, ice, smaller cup size, vanilla, Classic, sugar, extra espresso shots.

Recommendations

1. *Grande Americano* – a different cup of coffee.

2. *Quad, tall, Americano* – pack extra caffeine and increase the coffee flavor.

3. *Iced, venti, Americano* –a nice iced coffee on a hot day.

4. *Grande Americano* with steamed dairy – adds the dairy but keeps it nice and hot.

Low-Fat Options

1. *Grande, Americano* – it's just water and espresso.

2. *Grande, nonfat, Americano.*

Decadent Options

1. *Six shot, venti, Americano.*

2. *Quad, tall Americano* – packing it in.

Brewed Coffee

Ingredients: *coffee and water*

With all of the craziness around espresso-based beverages the most popular drink at Starbucks is still coffee. Just regular drip brewed coffee. You may notice that Starbucks drip brews through a flat paper filter, like you probably do at home.

You have several options when ordering a cup of coffee. Starbucks normally brews three coffees throughout the day. You can choose between bold, medium, and decaf medium-roasted coffees.

The offered bold coffee is rotated on a weekly basis. Some weeks you'll get Caffe Verona, other weeks it may be Sumatra. When there's a promotional coffee, regardless of its intensity, it may replace the bold offering. It could be for only a week or as long as a month. A good example of this would be Christmas blend – usually offered for the month of December.

The medium offerings, both regular and decaf, are always Pike Place Roast. As far as Starbucks coffee intensities are concerned it's the middle-of-the-road. It isn't very bold nor is it very mild. That's not to say that it isn't good.

If you want a cup of drip coffee then those are your options. However, you can also order a press-brewed coffee, coffee that's brewed via French press. If you choose the French press option then you can pick from any coffee in the store. You'll have to wait about five or six minutes for it to brew but you have a greater selection to choose from and the taste is sharper. If you have the time then that would be my recommendation.

Another possibility is to have your coffee brewed by the Clover.

The Clover uses Vacuum-Press technology. It's basically a reverse French press, although the technology is more complicated than that. What you end up with, all of the tech babble aside, is a coffee more vivid than even a French press can produce. When you choose Clover brewed coffee you have a select menu of coffees to choose from that are both rare and delightful. The Clover, and its coffees, are only available at select Starbucks stores.

Iced coffee is another option. The same blend is brewed every day – Iced Coffee Blend. It's simply regular or decaf. There aren't all of the options that come with hot coffee. It's a medium roast and most customers like it.

Of course you can add milk and sugar to your coffee. Those are located at the condiment bar. If you prefer soy milk just ask the barista.

A more unique way of modifying your coffee is to add espresso to it. If you want extra caffeine then you can add espresso at 75 mL per shot. If you add one shot then it's called a *red eye*. If you add two shots then it's called a *black eye*. I've heard that three added shots is a *purple eye* or *green eye*. I don't know about that. If you order a Purple Eye you'll probably just confuse the barista. Then again, maybe it would be nice to do that. Giving what you get!

You can also add a flavored syrup. At Starbucks none of the coffees have a natural vanilla or hazelnut flavoring like you find at some other coffee shops. By not roasting a flavor into the coffee beans the integrity of the coffee is preserved and you can still add the flavoring if you choose. Some choose to do this and those who do usually favor vanilla, hazelnut, caramel, and peppermint. Pumpkin spice is also popular in the fall.

Another option is a *Caffè Misto*, also known as a *Café Au Lait*. It's half brewed coffee and half steamed milk. You can always modify those proportions, and many do. It's good if you like a lot of milk and you want to keep your drink hot. Adding a little bit of foam on top is nice as well.

While it isn't very popular, some customers like to get a cup of half brewed coffee and half hot chocolate. I guess that creates a mocha of some sort.

Lastly, just so you're aware of your array of options, you can always order an Americano. It's just espresso and water so that gets it pretty close to drip coffee.

And don't forget, coffee and tea refills are exceedingly cheap if you are dining in the café. It should be somewhere around fifty cents. Take advantage of it.

Common Variants – Iced Coffee, Caffè Misto, Espresso.

Common Modifications – milk, sugar, espresso shots, vanilla syrup, hazelnut syrup.

Brewed Coffee

Recommendations

1. *Grande bold coffee* – the high test.

2. *Grande Pike Place Roast* – if you can't handle the high test.

3. *Venti iced coffee* – nice and refreshing.

4. *Grande, half hot chocolate, coffee* – what the heck, it sounds good.

5. *Grande Red Eye* – extra caffeine.

Low Fat Option

1. *Grande Pike Place Roast* – it's coffee, for crying out loud.

Decadent Options

1. *Venti Black Eye.*

2. *Iced, trenta, Black Eye* – don't do it.

Cappuccino

Ingredients: *espresso, steamed milk, foam*

Cappuccinos are very similar to lattes. They get espresso, milk, and foam. So what's the difference? The difference is they get what's called free poured milk. Free poured milk is steamed, aerated, and then poured immediately into the drink before it has a chance to settle. Once steamed milk settles the foam begins to quickly separate from the liquid milk.

A latte isn't free poured. Either the milk is allowed to settle or the foam is held back with a spoon when poured. When properly made a cappuccino should be lighter than a latte and should settle into about half milk and half foam after it's poured. A cappuccino is also creamier because of the additional foam.

The taste is very similar to a latte. However, there are a couple differences. For one, the texture of a cappuccino is creamier because of the extra foam. Foam lovers are usually big on cappuccinos. Also, the coffee flavor is stronger because the espresso is diluted with less milk. And, just like with lattes, if you like coffee and milk there's a good chance you will like a cappuccino.

All latte modifiers hold true for cappuccinos as well: decaf, extra espresso, various milk options, various syrup options, and all the rest. Be that as it may, it's not common to add syrup to a cappuccino. I've never seen anyone drink a raspberry cappuccino but you can. I think that's probably because a different type of person drinks cappuccinos as compared to lattes. A lot of latte drinkers like sweet drinks. That's not the same for cappuccino drinkers.

However, I'll qualify some of these modifiers because there are some slight differences. If you're thinking about adding syrup you should note that a cappuccino is made with the same amount of syrup as a latte. But it has half the amount of milk as a latte so it'll be much sweeter. So if you like grande vanilla lattes and you want to try a grande vanilla cappuccino, you might find that the vanilla is too sweet since it's not quite as diluted. I recommend cutting the syrup in half and going from there.

The most common cappuccino modifications are *wet* and *dry*. Maybe you like a little extra foam but you don't want your drink to be half foam. You can order your cappuccino *wet*. That means more milk than foam. If the milk to foam ratio in a cappuccino is normally about 50/50 then in a wet cappuccino it's probably 70/30. Another way of ordering a wet cappuccino is to order a latte with extra foam. It's just semantics. In both cases you'll end up getting a drink that's about 2/3 milk and 1/3 foam.

Dry means extra foam. Order this and you're going to get a drink that is mostly foam. It'll end up being about 30/70, milk to foam. Order it *bone dry* and you'll get a drink that has very little milk and almost all foam. Kind of like an espresso macchiato with extra, extra, extra foam.

A dry cappuccino is one of the more difficult drinks to make because the milk needs to be aerated properly to generate enough foam. It can be tricky. Neither a wet nor dry cappuccino can be free poured because that results in roughly half milk and half foam. A dry cappuccino needs to be actively aerated the entire time that it's steaming. It then needs to settle for a few seconds so the foam can be scooped off the top of the milk. It should be very light to the touch when finished.

Watch out for subjective terms such as *dry*, *wet*, *extra*, and *light*. I've seen confusion arise from these many times. The barista has his or her definition of what *dry* means but you and other coffeehouses might have different definitions. Make sure that you and your barista are on the same page so that you'll be as satisfied as possible. If there's confusion try to get as specific as possible by giving a percentage. Seventy-five percent isn't subjective. This will help ensure greater consistency in your drink.

Lastly, I don't recommend this drink iced. Hot foam over ice? If you think you might like it then try an iced latte first. I don't know many people who drink iced cappuccinos.

Common Variants – None.

Common Modifications – wet, dry, bone dry, soy milk, nonfat milk, whole milk, sugar, vanilla, extra espresso shots, decaf, chocolate powder, cinnamon powder.

Recommendations

1. *Tall cappuccino* – the standard.

2. *Grande, whole milk, dry, cappuccino* – for foam lovers.

3. *Grande, half of the vanilla, cappuccino* – for the sweet tooth.

Low-Fat Options

1. *Tall, nonfat, cappuccino.*

2. Tall, one pump sugar free vanilla, nonfat, cappuccino.

Decadent Option

1. *Venti, whole milk, chocolate powder, cappuccino.*

Cappuccino

Caramel Apple Spice

Ingredients: *cinnamon dolce syrup, steamed apple juice, whipped cream, caramel sauce*

This is a really great drink that a lot of people don't try. Maybe it's just too different from all of the other beverages, or perhaps it's the fact that it doesn't have caffeine. Whatever it is it's worthy of a test. It makes a good fall beverage and it can be a nice change of pace from coffee. It's only promoted during the fall but it's available all year. It's also a great drink for kids.

Many times there is confusion about the apple juice. Some mistakenly believe it's apple cider but it isn't. It's apple juice. This probably stems from the fact that this beverage used to be called *Caramel Apple Cider*.

It's starts with cinnamon dolce syrup, then steamed apple juice is added, then whip, and finally caramel sauce drizzled on top. Not surprisingly it tastes like sweet, hot apple juice. I find it hard to taste the cinnamon dolce in it but I taste the sweetness of it. The caramel flavor pairs perfectly.

In cold-weather markets it's often ordered extra hot. The whip melts quickly and the caramel sauce sinks right in. That also leads some people to order extra whip.

If it's too sweet for you try steamed apple juice without the syrup. That is an actual drink. It's called *Steamed Apple Juice*. You can also reduce the cinnamon dolce syrup and/or caramel sauce. If you choose to go that route I would recommend reducing the dolce syrup before the caramel sauce. Sugar free cinnamon dolce syrup can be substituted as well.

The most common modifier has to be extra caramel sauce. Caramel apples are good. I guess that's why extra caramel is good in this drink. I've never known anyone to order it iced but you certainly can.

As a side note there is a lot you can do with apple juice. Apple juice with chai syrup will make an *Apple Chai*. You can also use it with some milk or cream to make an apple Frappuccino. Caramel and cinnamon dolce syrups pair well in that. Or you can just order cold apple juice.

Common Variants – Steamed Apple Juice.

Common Modifications – without whip, extra caramel drizzle, less cinnamon dolce syrup, substitute sugar free cinnamon dolce syrup.

Recommendations

1. *Grande Caramel Apple Spice* – the recipe is good.

2. *Tall, caramel drizzle, Steamed Apple Juice* – if you just want some warm juice.

Low-Fat Options

1. *Tall, sugar free, no whip, light caramel, Caramel Apple Spice.*

2. *Tall, no whip, Caramel Apple Spice.*

3. *Tall Steamed Apple Juice.*

Decadent Option

1. *Venti, extra whip, extra drizzle Caramel Apple Spice.*

Caramel Apple Spice

Caramel Brulée Latte

Ingredients: *caramel brulée syrup, espresso, steamed milk, whipped cream, crunchy caramel topping*

This is a fairly new drink that has gained mainstay status and joined the annual holiday beverage lineup that also includes Peppermint Mocha, Eggnog Latte, and Gingerbread Latte.

It's made with caramel brulée syrup, espresso, and then steamed milk. It's finished with whip and a crunchy caramel topping. It can be ordered iced or as a Frappuccino.

If you've ever had caramel brulée then you can understand what the taste might be like. If not, I can tell you that it's a sweet caramel. Make sure you have a sweet tooth for this one.

There aren't too many crazy ways to modify it. If you like your drinks extra sweet then you can try adding caramel or toffee nut syrup instead of simply increasing the amount of caramel brulée syrup. Adding caramel drizzle on top is probably the best modification.

Remember, this is a seasonal drink. It'll probably only be around from November through January. However, if you want one outside of the holiday season you can get pretty close to recreating it by mixing caramel and toffee nut syrups.

Common Variants – Iced Caramel Brulée Latte, Caramel Brulée Frappuccino.

Common Modifications – decaf, extra shots, nonfat milk, soy milk, no whip, light whip.

Recommendations

1. *Grande Caramel Brulée Latte* – a holiday staple.

2. *Tall, soy, no whip, Caramel Brulée Latte* – for soy drinkers.

3. *Kids Caramel Brulée Crème* – caffeine free treat for the kiddies.

Low-Fat Options

1. *Tall, nonfat, no whip, Caramel Brulée Latte.*

2. *Grande, half the syrup, no whip, no topping, Caramel Brulée Latte.*

Decadent Option

1. *Venti, whole milk, extra whip, caramel drizzle, Caramel Brulée Latte.*

Caramel Brulée Latte

Caramel Macchiato

Ingredients: *vanilla syrup, steamed milk, foam, espresso, caramel sauce*

Say that one again. A caramel mocky-who? *Caramel Macchiato* (mock-ee-ot-ō). It's okay, you're not the only one that's been pronouncing it incorrectly for the last two years. You're accompanied by almost every customer that doesn't order it and a few who do. It's one of those quintessential Starbucks names that no one can pronounce. It's a staple drink. If you're looking for something to try then this is a good place to start experimenting.

It starts with vanilla syrup and is followed by steamed milk and a three-dollop bed of foam. Espresso gets poured on top of the foam and the caramel sauce gets drizzled on last in a secret pattern. Oooooo. And that's it. The iced version includes vanilla, cold milk, and ice. The espresso and caramel drizzle are poured in after.

The vanilla and caramel make it very sweet. It consists mostly of milk and foam but it doesn't get as much milk as a latte because of the extra foam. The foam, or ice, provides a cushion for the espresso and caramel sauce that lay on top, thus creating a layered drink.

One key here is the espresso is poured in after the milk, or milk and ice if it's iced, instead of before. In an iced caramel macchiato you'll notice that the bottom 2/3 is milk and the top 1/3 is espresso. You don't have to drink it this way. In fact I don't think many customers do. They mix it up.

If you like sweet coffee drinks then this one is right up your alley. It has caffeine and sugar. It's one of the most popular drinks, so if you've never tried one check it out. Fifty million caffeine addicts can't be wrong, right?

This is a heavily modified drink so let's dive into some common modifications. It's not common that people get less vanilla in their caramel macchiato than what the recipe calls for, even though it's too sweet for some. If you like the taste but wish it wasn't so sweet, then try less vanilla. That's my first recommendation. It'll reduce the sweetness but keep the delicious caramel sauce.

Extra caramel drizzle has to be the most common modification. People are crazy about the stuff. I can hear my wife in the background yelling "Oh yeah I am!" even as I read this aloud to myself.

Foam is another commonly modified feature. Many people ask for light foam, no foam, or more foam. Or just forget the foam altogether and get whip. That's good too.

You can also order it *upside down*. There's no hard recipe for constructing an upside down caramel macchiato. I've always made it with the espresso and caramel drizzle in the bottom of the cup. Many customers order it this way because it mixes up the drink better. I think some customers who order it iced get frustrated with the caramel sauce sitting on the top while their straw is sucking from the bottom. That's just my theory.

It's popular iced, and for good reason – it's refreshing. If you order an iced caramel macchiato upside down, or with extra caramel sauce, ask for some sauce to be drizzled on the inside of the cup. People go crazy for that. Maybe you will too. I don't know if they get any of that sauce because I think most of it sticks to the cup but they're excited to see it. It changes their whole mindset about the drink. Isn't that what it's really about anyway? Getting excited for your little treat?

Lastly, you can order it *skinny*. The connotation of skinny is that the beverage is sugar free and nonfat. However, ordering a skinny

Caramel Macchiato

caramel macchiato will get you sugar free vanilla and nonfat milk but it won't get you sugar free caramel sauce. Keep that in mind.

Common Variants – Iced Caramel Macchiato, Skinny Caramel Macchiato, Iced Skinny Caramel Macchiato.

Common Modifications – upside down, nonfat, whip, extra hot, no foam, extra caramel drizzle, caramel drizzle on the inside of an iced cup, light ice.

Recommendations

1. *Tall Caramel Macchiato.*

2. *Grande, upside down, Caramel Macchiato* – mixing it up!

3. *Iced, grande, Caramel Macchiato* – sweet and refreshing.

Low-Fat Options

1. *Tall Skinny Caramel Macchiato.*

2. *Tall, nonfat, light caramel drizzle Caramel Macchiato.*

Decadent Option

1. *Venti, whole milk, with whip, extra caramel sauce Caramel Macchiato.*

Chai Tea Latte

Ingredients: *chai syrup, water/ice, milk, foam*

Commonly referred to as a *chai*, this is easily one of the most popular drinks at Starbucks, both hot and iced. It's a staple throughout the year. There's also a lot you can do with it.

The hot version is made with chai tea syrup, hot water (about 190°F), steamed milk and a scoop of foam on top. It's about equal parts hot water and steamed milk. The iced version is made with chai tea syrup, cold milk, and ice. There's no water (ice substitutes for water) or foam. It tastes like sweet chai tea with milk. If you like chai and sweet things then you might really like it.

One of the most common ways to modify a hot chai is to substitute milk for the hot water. It gives it a heavier, creamier feel. That is ordering *no water*.

Want more caffeine? Additional pumps of chai will increase the caffeine content but also the sugar. You can add a shot or two of espresso as well. Adding espresso turns it into a *dirty chai*. Customers get a kick out of calling it dirty, especially those that order a *double dirty chai* (two shots of espresso).

Vanilla is a great addition. Many customers order *vanilla chai lattes*. Extra hot is another common modification. I'm not a chai drinker myself but there are an awful lot of chai drinkers who do get theirs extra hot. I think it comes with the tea territory. Soy is common as well. It's also worth noting that an *Iced Chai Tea Latte* is one of the quickest beverages to make. If you're ever in a hurray an iced chai won't take long.

Lastly, there is the *CHEG*, or *Chai Tea Eggnog Latte*. It's a Chai Tea

Latte that is made with eggnog instead of milk. Of course, it's only available during the holiday season. It's not very popular but it does have a small loyal following.

Common Variants – Iced Chai Tea Latte, Chai Tea Latte, Chai Crème Frappuccino, Chai Tea Eggnog Latte.

Common Modifications – no water, light ice, add vanilla, extra chai, no foam, nonfat milk, soy milk, add espresso, extra hot, less chai.

Recommendations

1. *Tall Chai Tea Latte* – this is a popular one.

2. *Grande, dirty, Chai Tea Latte* – for more caffeine.

3. *Grande, no water, Chai Tea Latte* – more filling, more flavor.

4. *Grande, soy, no water, Chai Tea Latte* – sweeter option for soy lovers.

Low-Fat Options

1. *Tall, nonfat, Chai Tea Latte.*

2. *Tall, half the syrup, nonfat, Chai Tea Latte.*

Decadent Option

1. *Venti, extra chai,* [specify number of pumps], *whole milk, Chai Tea Latte.*

2. *Venti CHEG.*

Cinnamon Dolce Latte

Ingredients: *cinnamon dolce syrup, espresso, milk, whipped cream, and cinnamon dolce powder*

Dolce is pronounced *dōl-chay*. It's a fairly popular drink. It's a latte so it starts with cinnamon dolce syrup and espresso but then milk makes up the majority of it. Lastly, it's topped with whip and dolce powder. The powder is a sweeter version of cinnamon. It's basically cinnamon and sugar. Cinnamon Dolce Latte is available iced. In that case it's cinnamon dolce syrup, cold milk, espresso, ice, whip, and dolce powder.

If you like cinnamon or you like sweet drinks then it's probably for you. If you've never tasted it it's essentially a sweet tasting cinnamon.

The most common ways to modify it are *no whip*, extra espresso shots, and *decaf* – nothing too crazy. There is a sugar-free cinnamon dolce syrup so it can be made skinny if you're looking to cut back on calories.

I should mention that cinnamon dolce is good as a syrup and crème drink. By that I mean the cinnamon dolce syrup with steamed milk and whip, but no espresso. That's a good kids' drink as well. Cinnamon Dolce Frappuccino is another popular variation.

Common Variants – Iced Cinnamon Dolce Latte, Cinnamon Dolce Frappuccino, Skinny Cinnamon Dolce Latte, Iced Skinny Cinnamon Dolce Latte, Cinnamon Dolce Crème.

Common Modifications – *decaf*, extra espresso, amount of syrup pumps, type of milk, *extra hot*, *extra whip*, no whip.

Cinnamon Dolce Latte

Recommendations

1. *Grande Cinnamon Dolce Latte* – the regular recipe is solid.

2. *Tall, extra whip, in a grande cup, Cinnamon Dolce Latte.*

3. *Kids Cinnamon Dolce Crème.*

Low Fat Options

1. *Tall Skinny Cinnamon Dolce Latte.*

2. *Grande, nonfat, no whip, Cinnamon Dolce Latte.*

Decadent Option

1. *Iced, venti, whole milk, extra whip, Cinnamon Dolce Latte.*

Eggnog Latte

Ingredients: *espresso, milk, eggnog, foam, nutmeg*

The *Eggnog Latte* is a seasonal drink, which is too bad because not only is it a customer favorite but it's also my favorite. It's usually available in November and December, right around the time of the holidays. While they certainly are not good for you, they are good. Oh so good. No one is going to pretend that eggnog is healthy so I won't either. But does it really matter? It's a seasonal drink so you can't drink it every day except for a limited time – thank goodness. And even health nuts have to indulge once in awhile.

It starts out with espresso and then you add a mixture of steamed eggnog and milk. After the mix is poured a little bit of foam is taken from it and added to the top of the drink. Lastly some nutmeg is sprinkled on. The mix is mostly eggnog but some milk is added to it to cut the strength. If it weren't, the drink would be even more unhealthy and the strength of the eggnog flavor would be too much for some people.

If you like eggnog and coffee then you'll probably like it. Be forewarned, they're addicting. During eggnog season I find myself drinking one almost every day. Subsequently I gain five pounds and my cholesterol jumps up twenty points. Nevertheless it's a festive and tasty beverage that many customers look forward to each year. Besides what's wrong with treating yourself once in a while, or every day.

There's always the common modifications but let me clarify a couple things. A nonfat eggnog latte only makes the milk portion of the mix nonfat, not the eggnog. Also, the portion that is milk is small so even when you order it nonfat you're still getting mostly eggnog. In light of all of that, nonfat eggnog isn't a real option. Just giving you the heads-up.

Sometimes it's lost that eggnog isn't a syrup but actual eggnog. I know I already mentioned it but I want to bring special attention to it. If the eggnog flavor is too strong for you then increase the percentage of milk in the mix or add espresso.

If you really love eggnog then you can order your latte made without milk and just eggnog. That's really good. Another option, to get more eggnog flavor, is to order fewer espresso shots. You'll be losing caffeine but that's the trade off. I like the grande and venti sizes with less espresso myself.

It is available iced but I recommend it hot, especially in colder markets like the Northeast. It just seems to be more popular hot. I don't think it's bad iced, it's just better hot. While I haven't given it its own outline, you can also get an Eggnog Frappuccino if you're looking to go cold with it.

Lastly, you can simply order a cup of *cold eggnog* or *steamed eggnog* if you want. A little steamed eggnog on its own is tasty. It's also a good kids' beverage.

Common Variants – Eggnog Frappuccino

Common Modifications – nonfat milk, extra hot, whip, no nutmeg, no foam, without espresso, decaf, without milk, extra foam,

Recommendations

1. *Grande Eggnog Latte* – it's great as is.

2. *Solo, grande, no milk, no nutmeg, Eggnog Latte* – my personal favorite; less espresso, without milk and nutmeg so you can get more eggnog flavor.

3. *Triple, grande, Eggnog Latte* – for extra caffeine.

4. *Steamed eggnog* – for those who simply love eggnog; no espresso or milk.

Low-Fat Options

1. *Short, nonfat, Eggnog Latte.*

2. *Tall, mostly nonfat milk, Eggnog Latte* – but what's the point? Seriously.

Decadent Option

1. *Triple venti, only eggnog, with whip, Eggnog Latte* – wowzers!

Eggnog Latte

Espresso

Ingredients: *espresso*

Espresso, as you've probably guessed, consists of shots of espresso. Nothing fancy here. It's coffee concentrate in layman's terms. It takes about eighteen to twenty-three seconds to pour a double shot of espresso. When made correctly it has a thick consistency and rich flavor. The top layer, or crema, should be a golden brown and caramelly sweet.

Espresso shots can be ordered in any quantity but are usually ordered in quantities of one, two, three, or four shots and served in a short cup. Remember that each shot of espresso is equal to one ounce and has about 75 mL of caffeine.

If you love rich tasting coffee then you might enjoy espresso on its own. If you just need a quick caffeine fix this is a great option. You can just pound it and go.

You don't have to drink it plain. Many people, who probably wouldn't care for just espresso, order shots and modify them to their liking. Adding sugar or dairy is one way to do that. I knew a customer who liked his with some eggnog – hearty and festive. You can also order shots in a cup of ice. They're great that way, especially in the summertime.

If you like the taste but don't think you can handle the caffeine then another option is to order espresso shots decaffeinated or partially decaffeinated. The caffeine content can be broken down almost any way you like.

Adding foam or whip to espresso shots are very popular modifications. Adding a dollop of foam will turn your shots into an *espresso macchiato*. Whip makes it an *espresso con panna*, or espresso with cream.

You can also order espresso shots *long* or *ristretto*. A long shot will have more volume, a weaker taste, and be more bitter. Ristretto shots are just the opposite. They are smaller, richer, and less bitter.

Lastly, all espresso shots quickly become bitter once poured. It's best to drink them right away or mix them with something else, like milk.

Common Variants – espresso macchiato, espresso con panna, Starbucks Double Shot.

Common Modifications – extra shots, decaf, half caff; with dairy, sugar, foam, or whip.

Recommendations

1. *Doppio* – it's the standard, give it a shot.

2. *Doppio with a splash of cream, on ice* – a refreshing shot of caffeine on a hot day.

3. *Doppio with a splash of eggnog* – a festive treat.

4. *Quad espresso* – if you need to pull an all-nighter.

Low-Fat Options

1. *Doppio* – it's just coffee.

2. *Doppio with a splash of nonfat milk.*

Decadent Option

1. *Six shot espresso* – ridiculous.

How to Order It

1 shot – *solo espresso* or *single espresso shot*

2 shots – *doppio* or *doubleshot of espresso*

3 shots – *triple espresso*

4 shots – *quad espresso*

With milk and sugar: *triple, [milk], [sugar], espresso.*

Espresso Macchiato

Ingredients: *espresso, foam*

Let's say you really like foam but you don't want milk. You can order an *espresso macchiato*. Espresso macchiatos are simply espresso with a dollop of foam on top. The term *macchiato* means *marked* in Italian. The marking was originally used by baristas to help waiters distinguish the espresso drinks that had milk in them.

In the case of Starbucks it's used to refer to a drink that consists of espresso shots topped with foam. It's served in a short cup and the default foam is two percent.

It tastes like what you expect: espresso and milk foam. When ordering one you should designate the number of shots that you want in it such as a *doppio macchiato* or a *triple espresso macchiato*. Ordering just an *espresso macchiato* will get you one shot.

Adding sugar and varying the type of milk foam are standard ways of modifying your espresso macchiato. However, many customers modify it by ordering a larger cup, maybe tall or grande. They fill the space with extra foam. Whole milk or breve is good if you want creamy foam. On the flip side you can order it *wet* and that'll get you a little bit of liquid milk.

Another variation is an *espresso con panna*. It means *espresso with cream* in Italian. Order it and you'll get espresso shots with whip on top. It doesn't have mainstream popularity amongst the customer bases that I've served but it does have an underground following.

Espresso macchiatos can also be modified with *long* or *ristretto* espresso shots. A long shot will have more volume, a weaker taste,

Espresso Macchiato

and be more bitter. Ristretto shots are just the opposite. They are more condensed, richer, and less bitter.

Common Variants – espresso, espresso con panna.

Common Modifications – decaf, extra shots of espresso, sugar, wet, extra foam, nonfat foam, whole foam, soy foam, with whip.

Recommendations

1. *Doppio macchiato* – standard and reliable.

2. *Extra whole milk foam, in a tall cup, doppio macchiato* – for creamier foam and plenty of it (get breve if you want to get even creamier).

3. *Wet doppio macchiato* – take some of the punch off the espresso.

4. *Double, extra whip, chocolate drizzle, in a tall cup espresso con panna* – it can serve as a delicious dessert. You'll probably want a spoon.

Low-Fat Options

1. *Non-fat doppio macchiato.*

Decadent Option

1. *Triple, breve espresso macchiato.*

Gingerbread Latte

Ingredients: *gingerbread syrup, espresso, steamed milk, whipped cream, nutmeg*

It wouldn't be the holidays without a *Gingerbread Latte*, would it? It's sweet and it's tasty, and it's only available November - January.

It's made by putting gingerbread syrup in a cup and then pouring in espresso and steamed milk. It's topped with whip and a sprinkling of nutmeg. It's also available iced and as a Frappuccino.

It's good. If you like gingerbread then you'll probably be a fan. If your kids like gingerbread then you can turn it into a kid's drink by cutting out the espresso and making it a *Gingerbread Crème*. If you've been a Gingerbread Latte fan for a while now then you'll remember the year that chunks of crystallized ginger replaced the nutmeg. That was bad. Funny, but bad. They sunk right to the bottom. Customers always asked what fell into their drink. I personally don't like nutmeg but I'm glad it's back.

It's usually modified in the typical ways: decaf, nonfat, extra whip. There's really not a whole lot of craziness here. However, there are a few noteworthy modifications. If you like chai then the chai syrup is a good addition. It's also true that gingerbread syrup is a good addition to Chai Tea Lattes. I guess it's a spice thing – spices with spices. Lastly, try substituting eggnog for the milk. It's almost the same as adding gingerbread syrup to your Eggnog Latte. It's pretty good.

Common Variants – Iced Gingerbread Latte, Gingerbread Frappuccino, Gingerbread Créme.

Common Modifications – decaf, extra espresso shots, extra syrup, nonfat, soy, no whip, extra whip.

Recommendations

1. *Grande Gingerbread Latte* – get festive.

2. *Triple, grande, no nutmeg, Gingerbread Latte* – for extra caffeine and coffee flavor.

3. *Kids Gingerbread Crème.*

Low-Fat Option

1. *Tall, nonfat, no whip, Gingerbread Latte.*

Decadent Option

1. *Venti, extra gingerbread, whole milk, extra whip, Gingerbread Latte* – splurge once in awhile.

2. *Venti, eggnog, Gingerbread Latte* – getting in the holiday spirit.

Green Tea Latte

Ingredients: *Classic syrup, green tea matcha powder, milk, foam*

This is a tough drink to explain. It's kind of an obscure beverage since it isn't very popular. But if you like green tea you might really like this one. It does have its own little cult following though.

The hot version is made with Classic syrup, green tea matcha powder, steamed milk, and a dollop of foam. The green tea powder is steamed right into the milk. It steams in quite easily and makes the milk nice and creamy. That should be a good thing. However, if you don't like foam it might work against you since the powder makes this drink so creamy, or foamy. It's difficult to make without foam.

You can get it hot or iced, like most other beverages, but it's probably better hot. It's made with Classic syrup, green tea powder, milk, and then a scoop of foam on top. The iced version consists of Classic syrup, cold milk, green tea matcha powder, and ice. The powder is stirred in. It can be difficult to get the powder completely stirred into the milk. I think it's better hot because you're more likely to get a consistent drink. Those who like hot green tea with milk will probably like it the best. If you're looking for a Frappuccino it's available in that form as well.

The most common modification with this drink is the milk – nonfat, whole, or soy instead of the default 2% milk. Other than that sometimes you'll see customers order it with extra matcha powder or without the sweetener. If you are thinking about adding a flavor to it then I recommend raspberry. It's a natural pairing. Any flavor that you add will be substitute for the Classic. Give this drink a shot, if for no other reason than it's fun to say "Matcha!"

Common Variants – Iced Green Tea Latte, Green Tea Frappuccino.

Common Modifications – no sweetener, extra hot, extra green tea matcha powder, no foam, nonfat milk, soy milk.

Recommendations

1. *Grande, soy, Green Tea Latte* – for soy lovers.

2. *Grande, no Classic, Green Tea Latte* – if you like tea but don't like it sweet.

3. *Grande, dirty, Green Tea Latte* – I've never heard of anyone adding a shot of espresso to this drink but if you love caffeine then what the heck, do it!

Low Fat Options

1. *Tall, nonfat, Green Tea Latte.*

2. *Tall, no classic, nonfat, Green Tea Latte.*

Decadent Option

1. *Venti, raspberry, whole milk, extra matcha powder, with whip, Green Tea Latte.*

Hot Chocolate

Ingredients: *chocolate syrup, vanilla syrup, steamed milk, whipped cream, chocolate drizzle*

Who doesn't like hot chocolate? Seriously, everyone drinks it at least once in a while. At Starbucks it's not only a favorite with kids but adults as well. That's not just because it's an old staple. It's partially due to the fact that you can modify it so many different ways.

Let's start with your basic hot chocolate. Everyone probably assumes that a hot chocolate gets chocolate syrup but at Starbucks it also gets vanilla syrup. Not a lot, just a little. It's not made with hot water either but with steamed milk. Of course it gets whip on top along with a little bit of chocolate drizzle (syrup). There it is – your basic hot chocolate.

There's not much you can really do here with ice. I guess you can make an iced hot chocolate. I can recall one customer who loved that. However, an iced hot chocolate is really nothing but chocolate milk with whip and a hint of vanilla.

It's worth noting that the chocolate syrup is a little thicker than most syrups so if you find that your hot chocolate is regularly not hot enough then order it extra hot. Additionally, you may want to ask for it stirred if the chocolate syrup is pooling on the bottom.

There are many ways to modify hot chocolate. If you order your hot chocolate without whip then you'll probably get foam as a substitute. If you don't want whip or foam then specify that.

If you like really creamy hot chocolate then try it with breve. I know you probably think it's gross to make hot chocolate with half

133

and half but just try it. It's delicious. Since the fat content is quite high, obviously, I recommend getting a short size. It's so rich and creamy that it's about all I can handle anyway. It's one of my favorite drinks, hands down.

One of the best ways to modify hot chocolate is to add a complimentary flavor. Some of the best flavors include: raspberry, caramel, peppermint, toffee nut, and white chocolate. Other good flavors that Starbucks doesn't carry year round but does from time to time, are: coconut and cherry. Ask if there are any promotional flavors available. Peppermint, caramel, and raspberry are generally the most popular pairings. Toffee nut and white chocolate are underrated but they're very good. If you add one of these flavors you're still going to be get vanilla. If you want to cut back on some sugar ask the barista to omit the vanilla. Your drink will be just fine without it.

The *Salted Caramel Hot Chocolate* is an excellent variation. It's made with chocolate syrup, toffee nut syrup, vanilla syrup, steamed milk, whip, caramel sauce, and sea salt. I have to admit that I was skeptical at first. It might be really sweet, but it is ridiculously delicious. It kind of tastes like a liquid Snickers bar. It's only promoted during the holidays and the winter but you can get it anytime of the year. The only ingredient that might be missing during the off-season is the sea salt. If you really like the sea salt then you can bring your own. It does add a nice element.

Caramel with hot chocolate is a really good combination. There are a couple of ways to make it. The traditional way is to mix caramel syrup in the hot chocolate. Another way is to add caramel drizzle, or sauce, on top. If I had to choose that's the way I would go – caramel sauce drizzled on top. So if you want a caramel hot chocolate specify which version you would like.

As stated above, *white hot chocolate* is also in play. This includes white chocolate, steamed milk, and whip. The white chocolate syrup is thick like the regular, so remember those advisories.

You can construct some other beverages with the white chocolate as well. For starters, you can add white chocolate to your hot chocolate. There are a few names for this: Black and White Hot Chocolate, Black-tie Hot Chocolate, Tuxedo Hot Chocolate, Penguin Hot Chocolate, and Zebra Hot Chocolate. If you like milk and white chocolate then this might be the combination for you.

Common Variants – Peppermint Hot Chocolate, Salted Caramel Hot Chocolate, Raspberry Hot Chocolate, Caramel Hot Chocolate, White Hot Chocolate, Black and White Hot Chocolate.

Common Modifications – caramel sauce, nonfat milk, whole milk, without whip, extra hot, extra chocolate, without vanilla, extra whip.

Recommendations

1. *Grande, with caramel drizzle, hot chocolate.*

2. *Tall, Peppermint Hot Chocolate* – tasty and sweet .

3. *Short, breve, no whip, hot chocolate* – just give it a try, trust me; I don't get whip because the foam is delish.

4. *Tall, raspberry, Hot Chocolate.*

5. *Kids hot chocolate.*

Low-Fat Options

1. *Tall, nonfat, no whip, hot chocolate.*

Hot Chocolate

2. *Tall, half the chocolate, no vanilla, nonfat, no whip, hot chocolate.*

Decadent Options

1. *Venti, whole milk Salted Caramel Hot Chocolate* – wow.

2. *Grande, caramel, extra caramel drizzle, extra whip, in a venti cup, hot chocolate.*

3. *Venti Peppermint Hot Chocolate.*

Hot Tea

Ingredients: *tea leaves and water*

After water, tea is the most popular drink in the world. It is believed that up to twenty billion cups of tea are consumed every single day. Tea is also incredibly good for you because of its high antioxidant count. So if you aren't drinking it then you should start.

Starbucks offers a variety of black, green, and herbal teas. You should also know that Starbucks offers the Tazo brand line of teas in a full leaf format. Full leaf teas tend to be more flavorful.

Of course, you can always modify your tea with milk and sugar. Though aside from that there are a few ways to snazz it up. You can add or subtract teabags or mix and match different teas.

One popular variation is a *Tea Misto*, or *Tisto*. Tea Mistos are like Caffè Mistos. They are half hot water and half steamed milk. You can add foam if you would like.

Take it one step further and you can make your tea into a tea latte. Tea lattes generally include syrup flavoring, tea, hot water, steamed milk, and foam. You can have any kind of tea in your tea latte that you choose but three have been promoted from time to time. They are *Black Tea Latte*, *Earl Grey Tea Latte* (a.k.a. *London Fog*), and *Vanilla Rooibos Tea Latte*. They include Classic, vanilla, and Classic syrup respectively.

They're commonly modified by adjusting the syrup, milk, and water content. On top of this, you may have noticed a couple of things. While Chai Tea Lattes are traditionally made with a chai syrup you can also make a Chai Tea Latte with a chai tea bag. It won't be as flavorful but it won't be as sweet either.

Hot Tea

You might also notice that, aside from the syrup, a Tea Misto and a tea latte are basically the same thing, aside from the syrup. Well, that's true, they are. Mistos and lattes are both good ways to spice up your tea if you're looking to do so.

Common Variations – Tea Misto, tea latte, iced tea, iced tea with lemonade.

Common Modifications – milk, sugar, syrup, additional tea bags.

Recommendations

1. *Grande China Green Tips tea* – high antioxidant content.

2. *Grande, no syrup, whole milk, no water, Black Tea Latte* - one of my faves.

3. *Tall London Fog* – just try it for the name.

Low-Fat Options

1. Any hot tea.

2. *Tall, sugar free, nonfat London Fog Latte.*

Decadent Option

1. *Venti, whole milk, no water Black Tea Latte.*

Iced Tea / Tea Lemonade

Ingredients: *tea, hot water, Classic syrup, cold water or lemonade, ice*

Even more popular than hot tea are iced tea and iced tea with lemonade. They're ridiculously popular actually, especially when there is hot weather.

Iced tea drinks are very simple. They're just brewed tea with cold water over ice. They're mixed by shaking. Normally there are three options for tea: Awake (black), Zen (green), and Passion (herbal). The Passion tea is decaf because it's an herbal tea. You can have all three as themselves or mixed with lemonade. Keep in mind that there's sugar in the lemonade.

You can order them sweetened or unsweetened. Technically the teas are sweetened with Classic by default because that's the recipe. The Classic syrup is ideal because it mixes in so well. However, many customers don't like their iced tea sweetened so you'll probably be asked when you order.

It's hard to say which tea, or tea–lemonade combo, is the most popular because they're all so popular. The Passion Tea is kind of fruity and when it's sweetened and paired with lemonade it makes a very refreshing drink. That's probably the most popular with high school kids. But like I said, they're all good choices.

You can also combine the teas and come up with some pretty good combinations so that might be something you want to experiment with.

It's worth noting that the tea is brewed strong when it's steeped. When you order it it's combined with more water to bring it down

Iced Tea

to a normal concentration. If you want your tea to taste stronger then you can ask for less water or no water. The opposite holds true as well.

Raspberry is probably the best flavored syrup to add. It tastes great with all of teas and tea-lemonade combos.

Lastly, you should know that if you are dining in the café then re-fills are incredibly cheap.

Common Variants – Black (Awake) Iced Tea, Black (Awake) Iced Tea Lemonade, Passion Iced Tea, Passion Iced Tea Lemonade, Green (Zen) Iced Tea, Green (Zen) Iced Tea Lemonade.

Common Modifications – less water, no water, light ice, extra ice, Classic syrup, raspberry syrup

Recommendations

1. *Grande Green Iced Tea* – refreshing and healthy.

2. *Grande, Passion Tea Lemonade* – sweet and berry.

3. *Venti, no syrup, Black Tea Lemonade* – my favorite.

Low-Fat Options

1. Any iced tea without sugar or lemonade.

Decadent Option

1. *Venti, raspberry, Passion Tea Lemonade.*

2. *Venti, raspberry, Green Iced Tea Lemonade.*

Latte

Ingredients: *espresso, steamed milk, foam*

Lattes are pretty simple. They're just espresso mixed with steamed milk and a dollop of foam on top. That's it. By volume it's mostly milk. Remember, two percent is always the default milk unless otherwise specified.

If you drink a latte it's going to taste similar to a drip coffee with milk or cream. However, instead of a lot of coffee with a little bit of milk you're getting a lot of milk with a little bit of espresso. Espresso is very strong though. You can easily taste it and it still has a lot of caffeine. In the end, if made by the recipe, it should be about 10% espresso, 85% milk, and 5% foam, roughly speaking. There are also iced lattes. They're made with cold milk, espresso, and ice.

A lot of people prefer lattes. If you drink coffee you might like them. If you like the taste of coffee at all you might like them. And whether you like your drinks sweet or not you can modify lattes to your liking. They're versatile like that.

How do you modify them? Of course you can make them decaf, add extra shots, change the milk, and so on. One of the most popular ways to modify it is by adding a flavor. Vanilla is by far the most popular but you can also choose hazelnut, caramel, raspberry, peppermint, toffee nut, cinnamon dolce, and current promotional flavors. Also, feel free to specify the amount of flavoring and combine flavors.

Cinnamon Dolce Latte, Chai Tea Latte, and skinny lattes are popular variations. Skinny lattes consist of nonfat milk, sugar free syrup, and lack whip. Caramel, cinnamon dolce, hazelnut, and vanilla flavors can all be made skinny.

One of my favorite modifications is adding protein and fiber powder. It gives the drink a creamier texture and gets more protein and fiber in your diet. It also pairs well with vanilla syrup.

Common Variants – iced latte, vanilla latte, Cinnamon Dolce Latte, Chai Tea Latte, Skinny Vanilla Latte, Skinny Caramel Latte, Skinny Cinnamon Dolce Latte

Common Modifications – decaf, half-decaf, one or two extra shots of espresso, nonfat, soy, vanilla syrup, caramel syrup, hazelnut syrup, extra hot, extra foam, no foam.

Recommendations

1. *Grande, vanilla, latte* – it's popular for a reason.

2. *Grande, two pump vanilla, latte* – if you like vanilla but think it's a little too sweet.

3. *Triple, grande, latte* – for extra caffeine.

4. *Grande, soy, latte* – if you can't have dairy.

5. *Tall, protein, latte* – it's delicious and healthy.

6. *Iced, grande, vanilla, latte* – refreshing on a hot day.

Low-Fat Options

1. *Tall, nonfat latte.*

2. Add a sugar free flavoring (caramel, cinnamon dolce, vanilla, or hazelnut).

3. Order it skinny – nonfat milk with sugar free flavoring.

Decadent Option

1. *Venti, vanilla, whole milk, with whip, latte.*

Latte

Mocha

Ingredients: *espresso, chocolate syrup, steamed milk, whipped cream*

A *mocha*, a *caffè mocha*, and a *mocha latte* are all the same thing. At Starbucks it's routinely called a *mocha*. Generally, mocha is the mixing of coffee and chocolate flavoring. Specifically, the beverage is chocolate syrup, espresso, steamed milk, and whip. It's just like making a latte except you're adding chocolate syrup and whip. An iced mocha is basically the same thing: chocolate syrup, espresso, cold milk, ice, and whip.

A mocha tastes like a hot chocolate with coffee. It's fairly sweet. If you like chocolate and coffee you'll probably like it.

Most mocha modifications are the same as lattes: decaf, extra shots, different milk. There are a few that are noteworthy, however. By default a mocha gets whip. So if you don't want it you'll need to specify that. If you ask for your mocha to be made without it then it's probably going to get foam instead. If you have any foam preferences then you'll want to make sure you specify those as well. Also, mochas are extra delicious when creamy. Switching to whole milk will do the job. Breve will make it even creamier but that might be too much to handle.

Another thing about mochas is that the syrup used to make them is a little thicker. It tends to lower the temperature of the drink by about five to seven degrees. The milk really should be steamed about five degrees hotter to compensate for this. If your mocha isn't quite as hot as you would like this may be why. Just ask your barista.

Some great complementing flavors are peppermint, caramel, toffee nut and raspberry. Many customers don't know about the raspberry and therefore don't think of this pairing. Peppermint is probably the most popular, especially during the holidays. Peppermint Mochas also get some kind of chocolate topping – probably chocolate curls or chocolate drizzle. It varies. It's available all year, just not displayed on the menu all year. How excited are you now, Peppermint Mocha lovers?

Caramel is really delicious. You can add caramel syrup and it tastes great. Adding caramel drizzle is excellent as well. Heck, if you really love caramel, add both.

Another option is the *Black and White Mocha* (a.k.a. tuxedo, zebra, black-tie, penguin). It's simply a mocha made with equal parts chocolate and white chocolate syrup. If you like both and can't decide then here you go. A variation of this is the *Marble Mocha Macchiato*. It's made with white chocolate syrup, steamed milk, foam, espresso shots, and chocolate drizzle on top. Again, you are getting both chocolates with this option. Since it's a macchiato the espresso is poured in last and there is no whip.

Common Variants – iced mocha, Caramel Mocha, Peppermint Mocha, Iced Peppermint Mocha, Raspberry Mocha, Black-and-White Mocha, Marble Mocha Macchiato, Mocha Frappuccino, Peppermint Mocha Frappuccino.

Common Modifications – decaf, extra espresso, nonfat milk, soy milk, less chocolate, no whip, extra whip, no whip and no foam, extra hot, caramel drizzle, caramel syrup.

Recommendations

1. *Grande mocha* – the standard.

2. *Iced, grande, mocha* – the iced standard.

3. *Grande, raspberry, mocha* – a nice combo.

4. *Grande, Marble Mocha Macchiato* –not well known and underrated.

5. *Grande, Peppermint Mocha* – try it, it's great.

6. *Grande, soy, no whip, mocha* – for soy lovers and dairy haters.

7. *Tall, caramel drizzle, mocha* – simply delicious.

Low-Fat Options

1. *Tall, nonfat, no whip, mocha.*

2. *Tall, sugar free caramel, nonfat, no whip, mocha.*

Decadent Options

1. *Venti, whole milk, Peppermint Mocha.*

2. *Grande, whole milk, caramel drizzle, extra whip, in a venti cup, mocha.*

Peppermint Mocha

Ingredients: *chocolate syrup, peppermint syrup, espresso, milk, whipped cream, chocolate topping*

Peppermint mocha is a holiday favorite for many people. It's one of the most popular drinks from November to January. While it's a variation of a mocha, I decided to give it its own section simply because it's so popular. It's actually available all year long. So if you love it then you can get it every day of the year even if you don't see it on the menu.

It gets chocolate and peppermint syrup, espresso, then steamed milk, whip, and some form of chocolate topping. The topping has varied from year to year. It's usually chocolate shavings. Chocolate drizzle can always be substituted if you prefer it. The iced version substitutes cold milk and ice for the steamed milk.

It's very sweet. If you like that, then it's fine. If you find that it's too sweet then I recommend asking for half the syrup that is in the recipe. It has twice the amount of syrup that goes into a mocha or a flavored latte. By reducing the syrup to half the amount it'll still be sweet but not super sweet. You can always reduce just the peppermint syrup if that flavor is too overpowering.

A good modifier is peppermint whipped cream. It used to be part of the standard recipe. It needs to be specially made so you may have to wait a minute or two. However, you might find that it is well worth the wait.

Peppermint Mochas have, on St. Patrick's Day, been sold as Leprechaun Lattes. Usually they sport green whip when this happens. Other than that it's the same thing.

A Peppermint Mocha Frappuccino is another available option. Adding chocolate chips to it is an excellent modification.

Peppermint White Mocha is available as well. The recipe is the same except white chocolate is substituted. This too can be made iced or as a Frappuccino.

Common Variants – Iced Peppermint Mocha, Peppermint Mocha Frappuccino, Peppermint Mocha Frappuccino, Peppermint Hot Chocolate.

Common Modifications – soy milk, nonfat milk, less syrup, extra whip, no whip, decaf, extra topping, extra hot.

Recommendations

1. *Grande Peppermint Mocha* – get into the Christmas spirit.

2. *Grande, soy, no whip, Peppermint Mocha* – if you don't want dairy.

3. *Tall, half the syrup, Peppermint Mocha* – cut back on the sweetness.

Low-Fat Options

1. *Tall, nonfat, no whip, Peppermint Mocha.*

2. *Tall, half the syrup, nonfat, no whip, Peppermint Mocha.*

Decadent Option

1. *Venti, whole milk, peppermint whip, extra topping, Peppermint Mocha.*

Pumpkin Spice Latte

Ingredients: *espresso, pumpkin spice syrup, steamed milk, whipped cream, pumpkin spice topping*

This one is definitely a popular drink. It's a seasonal drink – a great fall beverage. Every fall for the last five years I've been hooked on them. Before I started working for Starbucks it was my favorite beverage. It's usually available September through November. If you ask you might be able to get it the last week of August and, if there is still some left, as late as April. That varies on a store by store basis. There have been years where my store didn't have any pumpkin spice after January and years where we had it until April. It depends on how much is sold and when shipments arrive.

It's made with pumpkin spice syrup, espresso, steamed milk, whip, and a pumpkin spice powder on top. If you like pumpkin then you'll probably like it. It has a nice smooth pumpkin flavor, not over powering. You may want it a little extra hot because the syrup is thick.

It's also available iced and as a Frappuccino. When made iced it consists of pumpkin spice syrup, espresso, milk, ice, whip, and pumpkin spice powder. You can try one of these options but I recommend it hot unless you're in a warm part of the country.

You also want it stirred. Before I started working for Starbucks I had that issue. Not all baristas stirred it and the drink wouldn't mix well. If yours is lacking pumpkin flavor then there is a good chance that it needs to be stirred.

As good as it is, there really aren't a lot of modifications. You can change the milk and you can take the whip off but there aren't a lot of wild modifiers that are popular. Chocolate syrup is a pretty

149

good addition. In the same breath, the lack of modifiers says a lot about the original recipe.

Adding pumpkin spice syrup to drip coffee is another good option, especially if you don't like lattes.

Common Variants – Iced Pumpkin Spice Latte, Pumpkin Spice Frappuccino.

Common Modifications – nonfat milk, no whip, less syrup, decaf, extra shot, extra whip.

Recommendations

1. *Grande Pumpkin Spice Latte* – the original recipe is perfect

2. *Triple, grande, Pumpkin Spice Latte* – for more caffeine

3. *Grande, half the syrup, Pumpkin Spice Latte* – not quite so sweet

Low-Fat Options

1. *Tall, nonfat, no whip, Pumpkin Spice Latte.*

2. *Tall, nonfat, half the syrup, no whip, Pumpkin Spice Latte.*

Decadent Option

1. *Venti, whole milk, extra whip, Pumpkin Spice Latte.*

Starbucks Doubleshot

Ingredients: *espresso, Classic syrup, ice, 2% milk*

This is the king-daddy-dog of caffeine fixes. It's the one that's sure to jack you up. You don't order this unless you're serious about your caffeine. The name is a little misleading because the grande and venti sizes have more caffeine than a simple double shot. And don't confuse it with the canned Doubleshot. This is different. You won't find it on the menu because it's been discontinued. But from what I can tell it has a legion of fans.

Classic syrup, ice, and espresso are added to a mixing cup. It's then shaken and poured into a drinking cup. Lastly, 2% milk, or the dairy of your choice, is poured over the top. When made correctly it should look like the espresso and milk are unmixed but slowly mixing. That's because the dairy is just poured over the top and not shaken in.

If you like espresso or just want a caffeine rush then you should try it. I'll caution that if you order a venti it may take slightly longer to prepare than you're used to because of all the espresso shots that need to be poured for it.

It's usually modified in three different ways: (1) extra espresso (if you can believe it), (2) remove the Classic, or (3) change the dairy. Occasionally someone will add a flavor to it but it's not that common. Some like to add iced coffee instead of the dairy. That's sure to up the caffeine content. I can even recall a customer who liked their Double Shot blended after all of the ingredients had been added.

Common Variants – Espresso, Iced Espresso.

Common Modifications – extra espresso shots, no Classic, half and half, nonfat milk, whole milk.

Recommendations

1. *Venti Starbucks Doubleshot* – the real deal.

2. *Six shot, venti, no dairy, with iced coffee, Starbucks Doubleshot* – super charged.

Low-Fat Option

1. *Grande, no Classic, nonfat Starbucks Doubleshot.*

Decadent Option

1. *Seven shot, venti, no dairy, with iced coffee, Starbucks Doubleshot* – this should be illegal.

Vanilla Crème

Ingredients: *vanilla syrup, steamed milk, whipped cream*

In some circles this drink is known simply as a *steamer*, or a *vanilla steamer*. At Starbucks it's a *Vanilla Crème*. It's made with vanilla syrup, steamed milk, and topped off with whip.

It reminds me of when I was a kid and my grandmother would give me warm milk with a little vanilla extract. That's basically what it is. So, if your grandmother ever did that for you that's what you can expect: sweet vanilla flavored milk. I guess that's why it's such a good kids' drink.

When modifying it keep in mind that any flavor can be substituted. It's really syrup and crème. That means you can have a Raspberry Crème, Peppermint Crème, etc. Vanilla is the only one that is popular but not the only one that is good.

If you want to make it creamier then use whole milk or breve. Two percent milk isn't too bad but nonfat milk doesn't cut it for this drink.

A common variation is the *Syrup Crème Frappuccino*. It's essentially the same thing except frozen.

Common Variants – Pumpkin Spice Crème, Syrup and Crème Frappuccino

Common Modifications – no whip, nonfat milk, extra whip, alternative syrup

Recommendations

1. *Tall Vanilla Crème* – it's good if you want to go to sleep.

2. *Kids Vanilla Crème.*

Low-Fat Options

1. *Tall, sugar-free, nonfat, no whip, Vanilla Crème.*

Decadent Option

1. *Venti whole milk, extra whip, Vanilla Crème.*

White Chocolate Mocha

Ingredients: *espresso, white chocolate syrup, milk, whipped cream*

White mochas are very similar to mochas. The only difference is that they contain white chocolate. They're not quite as popular but popular enough to be a regular component of the menu.

The syrup is added first, then hot espresso, steamed milk, and topped with whip. If you don't want whip then you'll probably receive foam. It's most popular in its hot form but can be made iced or as a Frappuccino well.

White mochas are usually ordered by those who like sweet drinks. A lot of flavors pair well with it. Chocolate, of course, is one of them but so is raspberry, toffee nut, peppermint, and caramel. Raspberry and peppermint are probably the most popular. Caramel sauce is good on top.

Most mocha modifications are the same as lattes: decaf, extra shots, different milk. There are a few that are noteworthy, however. If you're not getting whip then make sure you specify your foam preferences. Also, white mochas are extra delicious when creamy. Switching to whole milk will do the job. Breve will make it even creamier but that might be too much to handle.

Another thing about white mochas is that the syrup used to make them is a little thicker. It tends to lower the temperature of the drink by about five to seven degrees. The milk really should be steamed about five degrees hotter to compensate for this. If yours isn't quite as hot as you would like then this may be why. Just ask your barista.

White Mocha

Another option is the Black and White Mocha (a.k.a. tuxedo, zebra, black-tie, penguin). It's simply a white mocha made with equal parts chocolate and white chocolate syrup. If you like both and can't decide then here you go. A variation of this is the Marble Mocha Macchiato. It's made with white chocolate syrup, steamed milk, foam, espresso shots, and chocolate drizzle on top. Again, you are getting both chocolates with this option. Since it's a macchiato the espresso is poured in last and there is no whip.

Common Variants – iced white mocha, Iced Peppermint White Mocha, Raspberry White Mocha, Black-and-White Mocha, Marble Mocha Macchiato, White Mocha Frappuccino, Peppermint White Mocha Frappuccino.

Common Modifications – decaf, extra espresso, nonfat milk, soy milk, less chocolate, no whip, extra whip, no whip and no foam, extra hot, caramel drizzle, raspberry syrup.

Recommendations

1. *Grande white mocha* – the standard.

2. *Grande, raspberry, white mocha* – a nice combo.

3. *Grande, Marble Mocha Macchiato* –not well known and underrated.

4. *Grande, Peppermint White Mocha* – sweet and festive.

5. *Grande, soy, no whip, white mocha* – for soy lovers and dairy haters.

6. *Tall, caramel drizzle, white mocha* – simply delicious.

Low-Fat Options

1. *Tall, nonfat, no whip, white mocha.*

2. *Tall, sugar free caramel, nonfat, no whip, white mocha.*

Decadent Options

1. *Venti, whole milk, Peppermint White Mocha.*

2. *Grande, whole milk, caramel drizzle, extra whip, in a venti cup, white mocha.*

3. *Venti, toffee nut, whole milk, caramel drizzle, extra whip, white mocha*

White Mocha

Blended Strawberry Lemonade

Ingredients: *strawberry sauce, lemonade, Classic syrup, ice*

This drink is unlike any other. It's blended but the recipe doesn't include any coffee, milk, base syrup, protein powder, or bananas – core ingredients for Frappuccinos and smoothies. It's made by blending strawberry sauce, lemonade, Classic syrup, and ice together. Then it's poured into a cup – no toppings.

If you like sweet and fruity then you'll probably like it. Kids usually love the sweetness of it but it's too much for some others. It's a bit tart. If it's too sweet then try cutting back on the Classic syrup first. You may find that you want to get rid of it altogether.

One of the best modifications is to substitute raspberry for the Classic. That adds an extra fruity flavor. You can make it even fruitier by substituting the orange mango sauce for lemonade, or simply adding it. Strawberry/lemonade, orange mango/lemonade, and strawberry/orange mango/lemonade are all good combinations. Strawberry/orange mango isn't bad but its consistency is a little thicker. Just keep that in mind.

There are a other non-Frappuccino components that are good blended. They include lemonade with any of the iced teas, apple juice with green iced tea, and strawberry sauce with passion iced tea. Adding Classic or raspberry syrup is a good way to sweeten any of them.

Common Variants – None.

Common Modifications – raspberry syrup.

Recommendations

1. *Grande Blended Strawberry Lemonade* – a real treat.

2. *Grande, raspberry, no Classic, Blended Strawberry Lemonade* – extra fruity.

3. *Grande, raspberry, Blended Strawberry Passion Iced Tea* – super fruity.

Low-Fat Option

1. *Tall, no Classic, Blended Strawberry Lemonade.*

Decadent Option

1. *Venti, raspberry, Blended Strawberry Lemonade.*

2. *Venti, raspberry, Blended Orange Mango Lemonade.*

Blended Strawberry Lemonade

Caffè Vanilla Frappuccino

Ingredients: *coffee, whole milk, vanilla bean powder, ice, coffee base syrup, whipped cream*

I think *Caffè Vanilla Frappuccino* is one of the best. It's regularly overlooked for Coffee, Mocha, and Strawberries and Crème Frappuccinos. I personally don't drink a lot of Frappuccinos but when I do this one is on my short list.

Frappuccino Roast, whole milk, vanilla bean powder, base syrup and ice are all blended together. The mix is poured into a cup and topped with whip. Basically, it's a Coffee Frappuccino with vanilla bean powder. You can also order a light version. That has a coffee light base syrup and lacks whip.

It's like a frozen vanilla latte. It has a vanilla and coffee flavor to it. Perhaps its best feature is the non-overpowering vanilla flavor. If you like Coffee Frappuccinos, Vanilla Bean Frappuccinos, or Vanilla Lattes then you might like this one.

There aren't any killer ways to modify this that I'm aware of. However, adding chocolate chips, chocolate syrup, a shot of espresso, or caramel drizzle are all good options.

Common Variants – None.

Common Modifications – decaf, nonfat milk, extra coffee, no whip, extra whip.

Recommendations

1. *Grande, extra milk, less ice, no whip, Caffè Vanilla Frappuccino* – one of my faves, extra thin.

2. *Single shot, tall, Caffè Vanilla Frappuccino* – extra caffeine.

3. *Grande, with chocolate chips, Caffè Vanilla Frappuccino* – chocolate and vanilla, what a combo.

Low-Fat Options

1. *Tall, nonfat, no whip, Caffè Vanilla Frappuccino.*

2. *Tall Caffè Vanilla Frappuccino Light.*

Decadent Option

1. *Venti, extra whip, caramel drizzle, Caffè Vanilla Frappuccino.*

Caffè Vanilla Frappuccino

Caramel Frappuccino

Ingredients: *coffee, milk, ice, caramel syrup, coffee or coffee light base syrup, whipped cream, caramel drizzle*

Caramel Frappuccinos, as you can imagine, are quite popular. It's made with coffee, milk, ice, caramel syrup and coffee base syrup (light base syrup for the light version). Those components are then blended. Once blended, whip (only on the regular version) and caramel drizzle are added.

It basically tastes like coffee and caramel. If you like Caramel Lattes, Caramel Macchiatos, or caramel and coffee in general then you'll probably like it.

Extra caramel drizzle is by far the most popular modification. You can also add extra Frappuccino Roast to get more coffee and extra whip is good too. If you don't want/like coffee you can drop the coffee and turn it into a *Caramel Crème Frappuccino.*

If you have a sweet tooth, then chocolate drizzle on top is an excellent addition. Chocolate pairs great with caramel. Adding a pump or two of chocolate to the blended components will also do the trick. If you're thinking about adding chocolate then another option is adding chocolate chips.

If you want to make your drink even lighter than the light recipe calls for you can substitute sugar free caramel syrup.

Common Variants – Caramel Frappuccino Light, Caramel Crème Frappuccino.

Common Modifications – extra caramel drizzle, extra whip, no whip, extra coffee, nonfat milk, soy, extra caramel syrup.

Recommendations

1. *Grande, extra caramel drizzle, Caramel Frappuccino –* everyone loves that caramel.

2. *Grande, soy, no whip, Caramel Frappuccino –* for soy people.

3. *Grande, extra coffee, Caramel Fappuccino –* for more caffeine.

Low Fat Options

1. *Tall Caramel Frappuccino Light.*

2. *Tall, sugar free caramel, Caramel Frappuccino Light.*

Decadent Option

1. *Venti, extra whip, extra coffee, chocolate drizzle, Caramel Frappuccino.*

Caramel Frappuccino

Chai Crème Frappuccino

Ingredients: *whole milk, cream base syrup, chai syrup, ice, whipped cream, and cinnamon powder*

The *Chai Crème Frappuccino* is the frozen version of the Chai Tea Latte. Whole milk, base syrup, chai syrup, and ice are all blended. It's poured into a cup and topped with whip and cinnamon powder.

It tastes like the Chai Tea Latte but a little sweeter. It also gets whip and cinnamon powder where the latte doesn't. If you like the latte versions then you might like this.

There are a few good ways to alter it. The most common way is to add more chai syrup. I'm not a chai guy but a lot of people seem to like that. Cinnamon dolce and gingerbread syrups pair well. Of course, making the chai dirty by adding espresso is somewhat popular. However, if you're looking to add coffee to it you might want to try the Frappuccino Roast instead of an espresso shot. A little bit of caramel drizzle on top isn't too bad either.

Common Variants – Chai Tea Latte, Iced Chai Tea Latte, Chai Eggnog Frappuccino (or CHEG Frappuccino)

Common Modifications – no whip, extra chai, nonfat milk, espresso shots

Recommendations

1. *Venti, extra chai, Chai Crème Frappuccino* – for more flavor.

2. *Grande, Frappuccino Roast, Chai Crème Frappuccino* – add some caffeine.

Low-Fat Options

1. *Tall, nonfat, no whip, Chai Crème Frappuccino.*

2. *Tall, less chai, nonfat, no whip, Chai Crème Frappuccino.*

Decadent Option

1. *Venti, double dirty, cinnamon dolce, extra whip Chai Crème Frappuccino.*

2. *Venti CHEG Frappuccino.*

Chai Crème Frappuccino

Coffee Frappuccino

Ingredients: *coffee, milk, ice, coffee or coffee light base syrup*

Many customers will name a Frappuccino as their favorite Starbucks beverage. The *Coffee Frappuccino* is the flagship drink of the product line and the foundation for the rest of the coffee-based Frappuccinos.

It's actually a very basic drink. It gets coffee, milk, ice, and then a sweet base syrup. All of the ingredients get blended together and the result is a creamy and frozen coffee treat. The regular version is made with whole milk as the default and the light version is made with nonfat milk. Neither of them get whip but it's common for customers to add it. Soy is popular too and gets made in a separate pitcher so you don't have to worry about cross contamination if you have an allergy.

It kind of tastes like a coffee milkshake but the consistency is a little different. It's icier than, and not as creamy as, a milkshake.

If it's too sweet ask for less of the base syrup. If the consistency is too thin for you then ask for more ice and/or less milk. If it's too thick then just ask for the opposite: less ice and/or more milk. You can also ask for it double blended. I think less ice and/or more milk is the best solution. The prevailing solution for thinning a Frappuccino seems to be double blending. I've never felt that that worked well.

If you want more caffeine, or coffee flavoring, then add more Frappuccino Roast or espresso shots. If you decide you to add espresso you can either have the shot blended into the drink or laid on top, affogato style. Hot espresso will thin the drink a little. I'd recommend extra Frappuccino Roast before trying espresso.

Common Variants – Espresso Frappuccino.

Common Modifications – extra coffee, nonfat milk, soy milk, whip, extra ice, espresso.

Recommendations

1. *Grande Coffee Frappuccino* – it's delicious.

2. *Grande, extra coffee, Coffee Frappuccino* – for extra caffeine.

3. *Grande, tall scoop size of ice, extra milk, in a venti. cup, Coffee Frappuccino* – making it thinner.

Low Fat Options

1. *Tall, nonfat, Coffee Frappuccino.*

2. *Tall Coffee Frappuccino Light.*

Decadent Option

1. *Venti, with whip, Coffee Frappuccino.*

Coffee Frappuccino

Double Chocolaty Chip Frappuccino

Ingredients: *milk, chocolate syrup, chocolate chips, ice, crème base syrup, whipped cream, chocolate drizzle*

This Frappuccino is perfect for those who like chocolate and don't like coffee. This makes it an ideal drink for kids, and a lot of them love it. It's essentially a Java Chip Frappuccino without coffee.

It's made by blending milk, chocolate syrup, chocolate chips, syrup base, and ice together. Then it's poured into a cup and topped with whip and chocolate drizzle. Fairly simple.

I don't really know what to compare its taste to, maybe chocolate ice cream with chocolate chips and syrup. It's a chocolate lover's dream – put it that way. If your favorite hot drink is hot chocolate and you're looking for a frozen drink then this might be a winner.

It's commonly modified by increasing the amount of chocolate chips, chocolate syrup, chocolate drizzle, or whip. Asking for additional chocolate drizzle on the inside the cup is another good modification for extra chocolate. Adding a secondary flavor is good way to spice it up if you're looking for more than extra chocolate. Caramel, raspberry, white mocha, hazelnut, toffee nut, peppermint, pumpkin spice, and vanilla bean powder all pair well. Everything pairs well with chocolate, doesn't it? You can also cut back on some of the milk and add strawberry sauce – delicious.

Lastly, if you're buying for two small kids you can always purchase one tall and ask for it divided into two cups. It's still plenty.

Common Variants – None.

Common Modifications – extra chips, extra chocolate syrup or drizzle, extra whip, light whip, no whip, additional flavor.

Recommendations

1. *Grande Double Chocolaty Chip Frappuccino* – the basic.

2. *Grande, chocolate drizzle on the inside of the cup, Double Chocolaty Chip Frappuccino* – some extra chocolate.

3. *Grande, half the milk, with strawberry sauce, Double Chocolaty Chip Frappuccino* – wow.

Low-Fat Options

1. *Tall, nonfat, no whip, Double Chocolaty Chip Frappuccino.*

2. *Tall, nonfat, less chocolate, no whip, Double Chocolaty Chip Frappuccino.*

Decadent Option

1. *Venti, extra chocolate, extra chips, extra whip, with caramel drizzle, Double Chocolaty Chip Frappuccino.*

Double Chocolaty Chip Frappuccino

Espresso Frappuccino

Ingredients: *Frappuccino Roast, whole milk, espresso, ice, base syrup*

If you order an *Espresso Frappuccino*, then it's probably because you need caffeine. It'll get the job done, alright. Here's how it works:

Coffee, whole milk, espresso, ice, and coffee base syrup all get blended together and poured into your cup. There are no toppings, not even whip. It includes two kinds of coffee: Frappuccino Roast (the coffee in all coffee based Frappuccinos) and Espresso Roast. Essentially, it's a Coffee Frappuccino with espresso. You can also order it light.

Each size gets the corresponding amount of Frappuccino Roast but keep in mind that every size gets the same amount of espresso shots. If you order a venti know that you're not getting any more espresso than a tall.

You can always add a flavor to spice things up, and there are many that pair well: chocolate, raspberry, white chocolate, and caramel all do. However, seldom do customers add them. It's probably because they just want the coffee. With that said, the most popular way to modify this one is to up the number of espresso shots. Sometimes customers like to order their espresso shots *affogato*. This means the espresso shots are poured, or laid, on top of the beverage instead of being blended in.

It's also important to note that espresso changes the taste of the beverage. It won't simply taste like a Coffee Frappuccino with a stronger coffee flavor. It will have a distinct espresso taste to it. If you don't like that, but you want more caffeine or coffee flavor, then your best bet is to order a Coffee Frappuccino with *extra coffee.*

Common Variants – None.

Common Modifications – extra espresso, nonfat, with whip.

Recommendations

1. *Grande, affogato, Espresso Frappuccino.*

2. *Triple, grande, Espresso Frappuccino –* if you need a serious frozen caffeine rush.

3. *Tall, with whip, chocolate drizzle, Espresso Frappuccino –* live it up a little.

Low-Fat Option

1. *Tall, nonfat, Espresso Frappuccino.*

Decadent Option

1. *Triple, venti, extra coffee, with whip, Espresso Frappuccino –* look out!

Espresso Frappuccino

Green Tea Frappuccino

Ingredients: *crème base syrup, whole milk, Classic syrup, matcha green tea powder, ice, whipped cream*

The *Green Tea Frappuccino* isn't real popular but it does have a following. Most partners that I know don't like it but there are always those few customers that come in every day to have one. To the anguish of these devout fans, melon syrup was replaced by Classic in the recipe not that long ago when it was discontinued.

Milk, ice, Classic syrup, matcha powder, and base syrup are all blended together. The resulting mixture is poured into a cup and topped with whip.

It tastes like sweet green tea. I said that only a few customers get it but I'm also convinced that more would if they took the leap and gave it a try. If you like green tea or the Chai Crème Frappuccino, then you might like this.

There are several widespread ways to revise it. If it's too sweet then cut back on, or cut out, the Classic syrup. If you want more tea flavor it's easy to add extra matcha. The best flavor to add is probably raspberry. It pairs very well. Peppermint is a good, but not as common, addition. Chocolate chips and chocolate syrup aren't too bad either, if you like chocolate.

Common Variants – Green Tea Latte, Iced Green Tea Latte.

Common Modifications – extra whip, no whip, extra matcha, nonfat milk, soy milk, raspberry syrup.

Recommendations

1. *Grande, raspberry, no Classic, Green Tea Frappuccino –* a very good pairing.

2. *Grande, peppermint, no Classic, Green Tea Frappuccino* – mint goes well with green tea.

3. *Tall Green Tea Frappuccino –* give it a try.

Low-Fat Options

1. *Tall, nonfat, no whip, Green Tea Frappuccino.*

2. *Tall, no Classic, nonfat, no whip, Green Tea Frappuccino.*

Decadent Option

1. *Venti, raspberry, extra whip, Green Tea Frappuccino.*

2. *Venti, chocolate chips, chocolate drizzle, Green Tea Frappuccino*

Green Tea Frappuccino

Java Chip Frappuccino

Ingredients: *coffee, milk, chocolate syrup, chocolate chips, ice, coffee or coffee light base syrup, whipped cream, chocolate drizzle*

The *Java Chip Frappuccino*, like most Frappuccinos, is quite popular. Just as a Mocha Frappuccino builds upon a Coffee Frappuccino, a Java Chip Frappuccino builds upon the Mocha Frappuccino. The difference between the two is just chocolate chips and chocolate drizzle.

It begins by blending coffee, milk, ice, chocolate syrup, chocolate chips, and coffee base syrup together. Once poured into a cup then whip and chocolate drizzle are added. It's that simple. The light version, if you can really call any form of a Java Chip Frappuccino light, doesn't get whip.

It tastes a lot like a Mocha Frappuccino – chocolate and coffee. The big differences are the texture and chocolate intensity. The chocolate chips add more texture. The chips and drizzle add more chocolate flavor.

Kids like it. However, if you're ordering for your kid, then you may want decaf. If you don't want any coffee you can always opt for the Double Chocolaty Chip Frappuccino. It is essentially the same thing as the Java Chip but without coffee.

People don't usually get too crazy with the Java Chip. Aside from modifying whipped cream and coffee the most common modification is probably adding peppermint. That makes a Mint Mocha Chip Frappuccino. Raspberry and caramel are both good additional flavors.

Common Variants – none.

Common Modifications – decaf, extra coffee, no whip, extra whip, extra chocolate chips, extra chocolate drizzle, peppermint syrup, nonfat milk.

Recommendations

1. *Tall, extra chips, Java Chip Frappuccino* – chocolaty and sweet.

2. *Grande, extra coffee, Java Chip Frappuccino* – for some extra caffeine.

3. *Grande, caramel drizzle, Java Chip Frappuccino* –caramel drizzle is just so good.

Low-Fat Options

1. *Tall Java Chip Frappuccino Light.*

2. *Tall, no whip, Java Chip Frappuccino.*

3. *Tall, half the chocolate, no whip, no drizzle, Java Chip Frappuccino.*

Decadent Options

1. *Venti, extra chocolate, extra whip Java Chip Frappuccino.*

2. *Venti, peppermint, extra whip, extra drizzle, Java Chip Frappuccino.*

3. *Venti, extra coffee, caramel drizzle, Java Chip Frappuccino.*

Java Chip Frappuccino

Mocha Frappuccino

Ingredients: *coffee, milk, ice, chocolate syrup, coffee or coffee light base syrup, whipped cream*

A *Mocha Frappuccino* is very straightforward. It's made with coffee, milk, ice, coffee base syrup, and chocolate syrup blended together. It's then poured into a cup and topped with whip (the light version doesn't get whip). You can also choose whether you would like chocolate or white chocolate, that is, mocha or white mocha. It's essentially a Coffee Frappuccino with chocolate and whip.

It tastes like coffee ice cream with chocolate but with a different consistency. If you like hot or iced mochas, and it's a hot day, it might be your chance to try one.

One of the most common modifications is extra chocolate. The standard recipe has a nice balance of chocolate and coffee, so if you want to tip the scales and taste more chocolate, then by all means add some extra pumps.

Raspberry, peppermint, and caramel syrups all pair well with mochas when they're blended in. They've all been promoted as a seasonal or limited time beverages at some point. The most notable of these is the Peppermint Mocha Frappuccino, which is promoted every holiday season.

Adding caramel or chocolate drizzle are also good additions. If you really want to go heavy on the chocolate then you can add chocolate chips.

As with hot and iced mochas you can create a Black and White Mocha Frappuccino by mixing regular and white mocha. Some people just can't get enough chocolate.

Common Variants – White Mocha Frappuccino, Mocha Frappuccino Light, White Mocha Frappuccino Light, Raspberry Mocha Frappuccino, Caramel Mocha Frappuccino, and Peppermint Mocha Frappuccino.

Common Modifications – extra chocolate, extra whip, no whip, extra coffee, decaf, additional flavored syrup, caramel drizzle, chocolate drizzle.

Recommendations

1. *Grande, extra chocolate, chocolate drizzle, Mocha Frappuccino* – for chocolate lovers.

2. *Grande Peppermint Mocha Frappuccino* – what a great pairing.

3. *Grande, soy, no whip, Mocha Frappuccino* – if you can't have dairy.

4. *Grande Raspberry Mocha Frappuccino* – to spice things up a bit.

Low-Fat Options

1. *Tall Mocha Frappuccino Light.*

2. *Tall, nonfat, no whip, Mocha Frappuccino.*

Decadent Options

1. *Venti Peppermint Mocha Frappuccino.*

2. *Venti, extra whip, caramel drizzle, Mocha Frappuccino.*

Mocha Frappuccino

Peppermint Mocha Frappuccino

Ingredients: *Frappuccino Roast, whole milk, chocolate syrup, peppermint syrup, coffee or coffee light base syrup, ice, whipped cream, chocolate topping*

This is a frozen holiday classic. It's most popular in warm markets. No surprise there but, nevertheless, it's popular all around.

It's starts by blending together Frappuccino Roast, whole milk, chocolate syrup, peppermint syrup, coffee base syrup, and ice. The resulting mix is poured into a cup and topped with whip and some form of chocolate topping, usually chocolate shavings. The chocolate topping has changed from year to year. It's also the only component that isn't available year round. If you order the drink in the offseason you can easily substitute chocolate drizzle for the topping. At one point it was made with peppermint whip. It's not anymore but you can always request it. It's good, you may want to.

This is also available in a light version. The light version simply substitutes nonfat milk and coffee light syrup base and doesn't have whip.

Peppermint mochas are extremely popular. If you like them, then you'll probably like this as well. If you like mocha flavored drinks, (chocolate and coffee) but the peppermint is too strong for you (it is a strong flavor), then you can always reduce the peppermint and still enjoy the flavor of it.

There are many popular modifications from extra coffee to light whip – all of the typical ones. A more distinctive modification is adding chocolate chips. It makes it a Mint Mocha Chip Frappuccino. This is the same as adding peppermint to a Java Chip Frappuccino.

If you substitute white chocolate for the chocolate then you can create a Peppermint White Mocha Frappuccino. Dividing the chocolate syrup into chocolate and white chocolate is also a good. That gives you a Black and White Peppermint Mocha Frappuccino.

Common Variants – Peppermint Mocha, Iced Peppermint Mocha, Peppermint White Mocha, Peppermint White Mocha Frappuccino, Mint Mocha Chip Frappuccino.

Common Modifications – decaf, extra coffee, nonfat, extra whip, light whip, nonfat, soy, extra chocolate topping, chips.

Recommendations

1. *Grande, peppermint whip, Peppermint Mocha Frappuccino* – splurge.

2. *Tall, Mint Mocha Chip Frappuccino* – everyone likes chocolate chips.

3. *Grande, extra coffee, Peppermint Mocha Frappuccino* – extra caffeine and more coffee flavor.

Low-Fat Options

1. *Tall, nonfat, no whip, Peppermint Mocha Frappuccino.*

2. *Tall, half the syrup, no whip, no topping, Peppermint Mocha Frappuccino.*

3. *Tall Peppermint Mocha Frappuccino Light.*

Peppermint Mocha Frappuccino

Decadent Option

1. *Venti, chocolate drizzle inside the cup, chocolate chips, extra peppermint whip, extra topping, Peppermint Mocha Frappuccino.*

Smoothies

Ingredients: 2% *milk, protein & fiber powder, banana, ice, and either strawberry sauce, chocolate syrup, or orange mango sauce*

Formerly known as Vivannos, and then banana smoothies, now they are simply smoothies. I'm a big fan. They're tasty, healthy, and a nice alternative to coffee. There are three different flavors: chocolate, strawberry, and orange mango.

With smoothies there aren't any toppings. Everything is simply blended together: 2% milk, protein & fiber powder, a banana, ice, and whichever flavor you choose.

Chocolate Smoothies have a fairly vibrant chocolate flavor. Personally, I like less chocolate syrup so I can cut back on the sugar. It still has good flavor doing that.

Strawberry Smoothies are probably the most popular, and in my opinion, the best. I mean, come on, it's strawberry. Strawberry is always the most popular smoothie flavor. The same strawberry sauce that is used in the Strawberries and Crème Frappuccino is used here. If you don't mind adding a few calories then try adding a couple pumps of chocolate syrup. You know it's dynamite.

Orange Mango Smoothies are probably the least popular. Don't take that to mean they aren't good. They are. I think they're just overshadowed by the other two. Chocolate and strawberry are two popular flavors everywhere you go. A popular modification for this one is to add green tea matcha powder. It pairs well with the orange mango.

One of the most common ways to modify a smoothie is to change the amount of banana. It's an actual banana that is used so you

Smoothies

can request half a banana, a banana and a half, or none at all. They're good without banana. Another modification is to adjust the amount of protein and fiber powder. A lot of people will ask for less but I always like a little extra. And, of course, you can always add whip.

It's also important to note that as I'm writing this, the smoothies are only available in a grande size. Hopefully that'll change in the future.

Common Variants – None.

Common Modifications – nonfat milk, soy milk, more or less protein & fiber powder, more or less banana, green tea matcha powder, less ice.

Recommendations

1. *Grande Orange Mango Smoothie.*

2. *Grande, extra protein & fiber powder, extra chocolate syrup, Chocolate Smoothie.*

3. *Grande, with chocolate drizzle, Strawberry Smoothie.*

Low-Fat Options

1. *Grande, one pump of chocolate, nonfat, Chocolate Smoothie.*

2. *Grande, nonfat, Strawberry Smoothie.*

Decadent Option

1. *Grande, chocolate syrup, extra milk, extra banana, with whip, Strawberry Smoothie.*

Strawberries & Crème Frappuccino

Ingredients: *strawberry sauce, crème base syrup, Classic syrup, milk, ice, whipped cream*

The *Strawberries and Crème Frappuccino* is a tasty one. Strawberry sauce, base syrup, Classic syrup, milk, and ice are all blended together. It's then poured into a cup and topped with whip.

As you would expect it tastes like strawberries and cream. It's very sweet. If you like strawberries and sweet drinks then give it a shot.

If you don't like sweet drinks then there are ways that you can modify it. My first recommendation would be to replace or cut out the Classic syrup. There's sugar in the base syrup and the strawberry sauce so it will still be sweet. Another option is to cut back on the amount of base syrup. You won't lose any strawberry flavor by modifying these ways. The amount of strawberry sauce can be reduced but then you'll be losing the strawberry flavoring.

If you want more strawberry flavor ask for more strawberry sauce and less milk. That will add strawberry flavor and keep the consistency the same, for the most part. Simply adding strawberry will make the drink thinner.

The best modification, in my opinion, is to add chocolate syrup. You'll want to substitute it for the Classic so it won't be too sweet. Chocolate and strawberry – they pair so well. I can't understand why Starbucks doesn't promote that combination. At least in the time that I worked there they didn't. Anyway, it's dynamite. Give it a try.

Lastly, it's been said that adding some hazelnut or toffee nut kind of tastes like Cap'n Crunch cereal. I've never had it myself but it might be worth checking out.

Common Variants – None.

Common Modifications – extra whip, no whip, extra strawberry sauce, nonfat milk, soy milk, light ice.

Recommendations

1. *Grande, soy, no whip, Strawberries & Crème Frappuccino* – a popular soy drink.

2. *Tall, no Classic syrup, with chocolate syrup, Strawberries & Crème Frappuccino* – simply delicious.

3. *Grande, extra strawberry sauce, light milk, Strawberries & Crème Frappuccino* – for strawberry lovers.

Low-Fat Options

1. *Tall, nonfat, no whip, Strawberries & Crème Frappuccino.*

2. *Tall, no Classic syrup, nonfat, no whip, Strawberries & Crème Frappuccino.*

Decadent Option

1. *Venti, chocolate syrup, extra strawberry sauce, light milk, chocolate drizzle, extra whip, Strawberries & Crème Frappuccino.*

Syrup Crème Frappuccino

Ingredients: *milk, syrup of choice, crème base syrup, ice, whipped cream*

In a Syrup Crème Frappuccino there isn't a designated flavor. You pick the flavor that you want to add to the crème mixture, so all flavors are in play. There's no coffee so it's also a popular drink for kids.

It's simple: the milk, crème base syrup, ice, and flavor of your choice are all blended together. The resulting blend is poured into a cup and topped with whipped cream. Real simple.

Raspberry and caramel are probably the two most popular flavors. Vanilla might be good but then it's basically a Vanilla Bean Frappuccino except with vanilla syrup instead of vanilla bean powder. Chocolate is surely a good choice but then it's really a Double Chocolaty Chip Frappuccino without the chips.

You can sub breve, or half and half, for the whole milk if you want it to be creamier. Blending whipped cream into the drink will also make it creamier.

You can mix all kinds of ingredients to make the drink you want. Chocolate chips, matcha powder, vanilla bean powder, all the syrups, sauces, and drizzles are all possibilities so use your imagination. One good recommendation that I can give uses apple juice. Apple juice, dairy of your choice (I recommend whole milk), crème base syrup, caramel syrup, cinnamon dolce syrup, and ice will give you a nice fall beverage. Top it with whip, cinnamon powder, and caramel drizzle. I know it sounds ridiculous but it's good. It's liquid apple pie.

Common Variants – Syrup Crème, Vanilla Crème.

Common Modifications – various syrups, nonfat milk, no whip, extra whip.

Recommendations

1. *Grande, Raspberry Crème Frappuccino.*

2. *Grande, Caramel Crème Frappuccino.*

3. *Tall, cinnamon dolce, caramel, breve, apple juice, caramel drizzle, cinnamon powder, Syrup Crème Frappuccino.*

Low Fat Options

1. *Tall, sugar free caramel, nonfat, no whip, Syrup Crème Frappuccino.*

2. *Tall, sugar free cinnamon dolce, nonfat, no whip, Syrup Crème Frappuccino.*

3. *Tall, raspberry, nonfat, no whip, Syrup Crème Frappuccino.*

Decadent Options

1. *Venti caramel syrup, extra whip, caramel drizzle, Syrup Crème Frappuccino.*

2. *Venti chocolate syrup, extra whip, caramel drizzle inside the cup and on top, Syrup Crème Frappuccino.*

Vanilla Bean Frappuccino

Ingredients: *milk, vanilla bean powder, créme base syrup, ice, whipped cream*

Vanilla Bean Frappuccinos are a staple in the Frappuccino lineup. Many people like vanilla and it provides another caffeine-free option for kids.

It's made by blending milk, vanilla bean powder, créme base syrup, and ice together in a pitcher. The mixture is then poured into a cup and topped with whip.

It's sweet just like the other Frappuccinos. I think the best drink to compare it with is Vanilla Crème. That's the flavor that it's most akin to, except it's frozen of course.

Aside from canceling the whip, I seldom see this drink modified. With that said, I do have a few recommendations. Many flavors will pair well with this because it's vanilla. Caramel, raspberry, and chocolate are chief among those. Caramel drizzle makes a nice topping and chocolate chips can add a subtle chocolate flavor to it.

If you want to get a little crazier then add white chocolate syrup and chips. It'll create something like a cookies n' cream flavor. Lastly, adding white chocolate, peppermint, and either chocolate syrup or chips (or both) will create something like a peppermint patty. It might take some experimenting to get the proportions right with these two but you might find it worth the experimenting.

Common Variants – Vanilla Crème.

Common Modifications – extra whip, no whip, nonfat milk.

Recommendations

1. *Grande, caramel drizzle, Vanilla Bean Frappuccino* – is there any doubt that adding drizzle will be good?

2. *Tall, white chocolate, chocolate chips, Vanilla Bean Frappuccino.*

3. *Grande, chocolate, caramel drizzle, Vanilla Bean Frappuccino.*

Low-Fat Options

1. *Tall, nonfat, no whip Vanilla Bean Frappuccino.*

Decadent Options

1. *Venti, chocolate chips, extra whip, caramel drizzle, Vanilla Bean Frappuccino.*

2. *Venti, white chocolate, peppermint, chocolate chips, peppermint whip, chocolate drizzle, Vanilla Bean Frappuccino.*

Chapter Seven:

How to Order Your Beverage

"It usually takes more than three weeks to prepare a good impromptu speech." – Mark Twain

Customers always say that they don't know how to order their drink. They order it and then say "I know I didn't say that right." Hopefully these pages help you. I've listed the order in which you should speak modifications followed by some examples. It may seem overwhelming but remember: you probably won't need to modify every category. If you do, congratulations! You're one of only a few. Hopefully, after reading this section, you'll be able to order your drink like a professional customer.

When ordering your beverage you should state the modifications in the following order:

1. **Quantity of Drinks** – If you're ordering multiple of the same drink you'll state that first.

2. **Cup Type** – Iced or hot. If it's hot you don't need to specify but if it's iced you do. Frappuccinos are always frozen/iced

so you don't need to specify with them either.

3. **Decaf** – If you want your drink decaf, or some fraction of it decaf, then you'll state that next. It might be decaf, half decaf (half caff), or a quarter decaf. It can be any fraction that you want. All drinks are regular by default.

4. **Espresso Shots** – If you're modifying the number of shots that the recipe calls for then this is where you state that. Double, triple, quad, five shot, six shot, etc. Those are the terms to use.

5. **Size** – Size of the beverage

6. **Syrup** – The flavor of syrup that you would like added to your drink. For example, if you're ordering a latte and you're adding peppermint then this is where you would state that: grande, *peppermint,* latte. If you're only modifying the amount of syrup, but not adding a new syrup, then you only need to order the modified number of pumps. For example, you want a mocha but with less syrup. You would order it with *two pumps* or *one pump* as opposed to *two pumps mocha* or *one pump mocha.* It should sound like this: grande, *two pump*, no whip, mocha. The type of syrup is implied in the name of the drink.

7. **Dairy** – The kind of dairy that you would like in your drink. Again, you only state this if you're modifying from the original recipe. Most drinks normally come with two percent milk so if you want two percent then you don't need to state that.

8. **Other Modifiers** – Anything else goes in here: sugar, room, whipped cream, extra hot, specific temp, etc.

9. **Name of the Drink** – State the name of the drink here: latte, cappuccino, mocha, misto, Java Chip Frappuccino, etc.

Here are a few examples:

A. iced,   decaf,   quad,   venti,   raspberry,   non-fat,
   2   3   4   5   6   7

no whip,   extra ice,   mocha
   8   8   9

B. ½ caff,   venti,   extra hot,   2 Splenda,   latte
     3   5   8   8   9

C. tall,   5 pump,   soy,   no water,   Chai Tea Latte
    5   6   7   8   9

D. two,   grande,   extra whip,   hot chocolates
    1   5   8   9

Remember:
1. Quantity
2. Iced
3. Decaf
4. Espresso Shots
5. Size
6. Syrup
7. Dairy
8. Anything Else
9. Name of Drink

Chapter Eight:

How to Get Hired at Starbucks

"All I've ever wanted was an honest week's pay for an honest day's work." – Steve Martin

I have spoken with so many people who want to work at Starbucks. There's an incredible fascination with making all of those drinks. In fact, when someone gets hired they often want to rush right into making drinks. But hold your horses, there's a lot more to working at Starbucks than just making drinks. While making drinks is a popular reason it's not the only one. Benefits, career development, supplemental income, a part-time college job, a hobby, and a love of working with people or coffee are all common reasons.

In any event, it's true that at the store level Starbucks is a transitional job for most. There are a lot of college kids, kids fresh out of college, those looking to hone management skills, those who need benefits or extra income, and those who want to progress up the corporate ladder. Starbucks is a good place to work for all these reasons and a few more.

I guess the first question you have to ask yourself is, "Why do I want to work at Starbucks?" You need to know what you want to accomplish from working there and how Starbucks will help you with that. You would be surprised by how many people can't answer that question in an interview. Many times when I ask that question I get an awkward laugh followed by "Cause I need a job." That's a really bad answer, just in case you don't know.

Knowing what you want will accomplish and convey several things. First, you'll project preparedness and responsibility if you can articulate clear and attainable goals for yourself during the interview process. Second, you will advance yourself forward if you know what you want. You will improve yourself when you take purposeful action and complete your objectives. Lastly, you will help prevent yourself from taking the wrong job. When you are one or two months into a job and realize that it isn't for you it can set you back to square one. In the same breath, Starbucks doesn't want to use resources training the wrong person. Some of the most frustrating times were when my staff and I would spend two months training someone only to watch them leave. That is why you need a solid answer for this question before you apply.

The second question you have to ask yourself is, "What do I have to offer Starbucks and in what capacity?" You can't take a job without any thought of it or for purely selfish ambitions. The company that hires you is going to expect you to work hard to help them accomplish *their* goals. That's why they're willing to help you by paying wages, offering benefits, and providing a healthy workplace.

You might have more to offer than you think. Or you might think you have more to offer than you really do. To determine this it's important that you not only know what you can offer but what Starbucks is looking for as well. You might have extensive experience as an investment banker or a rocket scientist but is that what

Starbucks is looking for? You have to remember that it's a two-way street.

When the housing bubble burst and the economy tanked my store received many applicants just like these. I hired some but many times it was awkward for them and us. They didn't want to be there. Some quickly left after they found higher paying positions. It didn't take me long to stop hiring candidates like these because I simply didn't trust that they would stay.

Having clear answers to these two questions is more than just a tip on how to interview at Starbucks. It's advice that'll keep you from making a mistake that harms you and your employer, no matter what position you apply for. It's applicable to every job, not just Starbucks.

So what does Starbucks want from their partners and what skills are needed to succeed? Working in a Starbucks store requires a unique set of blended skills whether you are a barista, supervisor, assistant manager, or store manager. To succeed you need to be a team player, dependable, wise, coachable, personable, a good multitasker, available, and above all else, positive. You have to be all of those things. If you want to be a supervisor or manager then you have to be all of that and more.

I've probably interviewed hundreds of people and hired and trained over a hundred more. It's always the same skill sets that work and everyone always thinks they can make it work some other way. It really does take a special person to succeed at Starbucks.

In order for the store to function and provide the level of customer service that it's meant to every partner needs to possess all of those skills. Before discussing these skills, as well as those that are detrimental, let's first look at the application process.

Applying

When you've decided that Starbucks and you are a fit for each other, then you're ready to apply and see if they feel the same way. I should qualify something before I continue. When you apply you're only applying to one store. Every store manager is different, every store has different needs, and there are a zillion stores. Get the picture? If you don't succeed at one then you might succeed at the next.

As of 2009, Starbucks only accepts applications online. It changed the game. Managers used to get a "preview" of an applicant when they handed in their application. This quick first impression could go a long way when deciding who would get called for interviews. Now, with the advent of compulsory online application submission, that first impression is gone. Or is it?

Most applicants venture online, click *send* to submit their application, and that's the end of it. It then becomes lost in a black hole of applications. Some stand out of the pack but so many look the same that sometimes it can seem impossible to identify a good candidate.

This is where your opportunity comes in. Submit the application online and then personally take a cover letter and resume into the manager. A cover letter and resume? For Starbucks? Trust me, this will help you. Very few people submit resumes and almost no one submits a cover letter, especially one that's customized to the job.

A customized cover letter will convey that you're serious and on top of your game. Make sure you've done your homework on Starbucks and the position you're applying for. You'll need information like this to customize it. Generic cover letters can be spotted from a mile away. They scream "I don't want to make an effort!" If you're not making an effort now, then why should I believe that you'll make an effort when I hire you?

You don't need to go crazy with it. Keep it to just a page. Talk about why you want the job, how you're going to make the store better, and insert some info about Starbucks that will show you've done some research. Keep in mind that the upcoming list of traits and behaviors make great adjectives to stuff your cover letter and resume with.

You don't need a ton of experience to get hired at Starbucks but your resume is just as important as the cover letter. It also needs to be customized. Certainly make sure that it's updated and error free. To stand out you need to emphasize your customer service and retail work history (if you have it). This job is all about customer service. Give your experience some life by getting granular with the details. Most resumes are very generic with the experience that they convey. That says one of two things: 1) I'm lazy and don't pay attention to details (so I won't when I work for you either) and/or 2) I don't have very good experience so I'm going to dress it up by generalizing everything and maybe I'll get lucky.

You need to get granular. Here are some bad examples:

Excelled as a cashier.

Sales associate who helped customers and stocked shelves.

Try these instead:

As cashier I processed over 300 transactions and handled over $7,000 in cash daily.

As a customer service rep. my average monthly customer satisfaction rating (survey of 100+ customers) was over 95%.

See how the first two are so blah? You're either selling yourself short or hiding something. The second two examples provide a much better description of your performance. No matter how insignificant you believe your work experience to be you can convey it in stronger terms. To make your case even stronger you need to hand deliver this information.

When your cover letter and resume are ready for prime time then you can take them to the manager. This will give you an advantage over other applicants. Make sure that you speak with the manager. Don't leave your documents with someone else. If the manager isn't there ask when he or she will be and go back. Most managers are usually in the store on Mondays and most stores are quietest in the late morning and early afternoons. Again, every store is different.

Introduce yourself and let them know that you've already submitted the application. Don't be shy. Customer service is the most important aspect of a barista's job. I know a lot of managers who heavily weigh personality when they meet an applicant. They want people who are going to be friendly/personable/outgoing. Customers like those kinds of people. Make sure that you have that going on when you go into the store.

Now, let's assume that you've secured an interview. You need to orally convey that you're qualified for the job and will succeed in it. To communicate that convincingly you need to understand what it takes to succeed in the position. The skills I've listed are imperative for working at Starbucks. Assess and communicate yourself within them.

Availability

If you want to work at Starbucks, then the first thing you need to be is available. Each store has a complex arrangement of scheduled shifts. The more you are available, and the more that you can be scheduled, the more attractive you're going to be as an employee.

Sometimes a person will be a great candidate but their availability is inadequate. They're only available to work three hours a day or two days a week. It doesn't matter how great your skills are, if you're not available when the store needs you to be, then you're not a viable candidate.

Another perspective within the availability paradigm is longevity. How long do you plan to work at Starbucks? Are you just looking for summer employment? Is Starbucks just a holdover while you continue to search for a job in your field of expertise?

Summer employment doesn't normally work because it'll take a couple of months just to train you, that is, for you to get really comfortable in your position. The store management team can't be asked to put in the focus and work of training a new partner only to have that partner leave once they're fully trained.

The same philosophy goes for an applicant who is planning to continue searching for a job in another field. If you're planning on leaving once you find a job within your expertise then you should be upfront about that. Things happen and life changes but you should be intending to work at Starbucks for at least a year if you apply.

Dependability

When I think about dependability I always think about this one partner, Michael. Michael was a customer before he was a partner. All the partners loved him. He was a good customer and very personable. So when Michael applied I certainly felt like he would give great customer service. The problem, I quickly realized, was that Michael was not dependable at all. He would be late or not in dress code. When he was there you couldn't count on him completing his tasks.

One morning he showed up at 7:15 in a panic. He thought that he was late again so first he apologized for that. Then he went on to show me that the only shirt he had to wear was dirty and in a wrinkled ball. I then told him that he wasn't even scheduled to work that day. You should've seen the relief on his face.

If you're available then the next thing you need to be is dependable. It sounds pretty basic, being dependable. However, a lot of people are not truly dependable. Dependable means following through on commitments. It means consistently being on time for work, in dress code, awake and alert, and ready to perform the tasks that are asked of you in a thorough and efficient manner, all the time.

Being dependable is not an easy thing to do. It takes resolve, perseverance, organization, maturity and pride. You need to be committed to being dependable. It's not just something that you are or you aren't. It takes a special mindset and commitment to being that person that everyone knows is going to be there to get the job done.

Some people can never get to work on time, some people can never come to work in the right clothes, and some people can just never get the tasks done that they're suppose to get done. These people are not dependable. If you're available but you don't show up, then it really doesn't matter that you're available.

When you're dependable you're revered throughout your workplace. Not just by your boss but, just as importantly, by your coworkers. You're not just being a good employee but you're also leading by example. And a little bit of leaven goes through the whole dough. Unreliable people like Michael see your example and want to emulate it. A lot of people are counting on your dependability: your managers (store managers and above), your supervisor, your fellow baristas, and the customers.

Interpersonal Savvy

You need to be personable. That means you need to be a people person. At Starbucks you're not sitting behind a desk typing code and you're not in a lab handling test tubes. You're working face-to-face with your coworkers and hundreds of customers every day.

However, being personable means a lot more than just being friendly. Amongst your coworkers it means saying "Hi," asking about their lives, and getting to know them. This builds commitment and trust between you and those you work with. You can work just fine with people that you don't know or you don't like but people work better together when they care about each other.

With customers it means being friendly, perceptive, and generally cordial. You need to smile and greet them genuinely; candidly. It doesn't mean that robotic smile and greeting that you get at so many places. "Welcome to McDonald's, would you like to try a value meal? Welcome to McDonald's, would you like to try a value meal? Welcome to McDonald's, would you like to try value meal?" Don't you hate that? You can't tell if it's a person, a recording, or some kind of new robot.

You need to get to know the customers. You need to ask them their name, ask "How's Johnny doing in school?", and if Sally won her soccer game. I know it gets really busy sometimes, but you can't hand out drinks with your head down either. You need to make eye contact and pause for at least three seconds to have that interaction, even if it's for a simple thank you. I know you are at work, and you do see a lot of customers, but you are still a person. Besides, that interaction is your work. That's easily lost.

You also need to keep in mind that you don't know what's happening in everyone's life. When you meet a customer you don't know where they just came from. They may have just received the worst news of their life. The least you can do is make their interaction with you enjoyable.

Lastly, don't be *too* outgoing and personable. You want to be pleasant and charming but this isn't a social hour either. It is possible to cross the line. I've seen partners carry on a two-minute conversation with the customer at the counter while there are five people standing in line behind them. I've also seen partners who were so loud, and so bubbly, that customers would complain. Assess the situation and use some common sense. It will serve you well.

Wisdom

Wisdom doesn't mean a 1600 SAT score. It means that you need to use common sense and think situations through. You need to know what to do in all situations. Just as a baseball player needs to know what to do when the ball is hit you need to know when to do what. Intelligence is knowing how to do something. Wisdom is knowing when and how to apply intelligence. Before you say or do something think about the ripple effect that your actions could set off. Too many times people are careless. Just as often people try to do too much. It's one thing to want to help and work hard.

It's another thing to work so hard and do so much that you do too much. Your contribution then becomes detrimental to the store.

When you work for a company you are essentially being paid to represent them. So, when you put on a Starbucks apron you need to do what Starbucks wants you to do and not what you want to do.

Let me give you a good example. A customer tells you that you made their drink wrong and you don't believe that you did. What do you do? First of all, it doesn't matter if you did or didn't because the customer feels like you did. Ultimately, that means you did. You might have the urge to say, "No, it's right. I make it all the time." If you do that then the customer could perceive that you are arguing with them, that you're simply being difficult. You really just want to ask them why it's wrong, apologize, remake it as quickly as possible, and wish them a good day. Don't let your pride get in the way. You may know how to make the drink and how to apologize, but do you know when to do those things?

Stop and think about this for a minute. Let's say you really did make the drink right. What has bigger implications here: winning the argument or the customer believing that their needs were met?

Whether you are right or wrong is a moot point. What is the best that you're actually hoping for? That the customer will say they're wrong and you're right? What does that really accomplish? Besides, if they say you're right then they might be too embarrassed to ever come back.

Making the customer feel like you really care about them and their beverage has a positive and lasting effect. They believe you're honest. They recognize that you're human, that you make mistakes, and when you do you're concerned about correcting them. Customers who feel like that come back every day. That makes it a wise decision. Besides, you probably did make the drink wrong. If you're making four hundred drinks a day, and three or four at a time, then you're going to make mistakes.

What I'm really getting at here is the ability to think things through. It sounds so incredibly simple and trite but few people can interact like that, especially if it tests their pride.

Being wise means being a good decision-maker. No one is perfect but you shouldn't be careless or repeating the same mistakes either. Partners who gain wisdom by learning from their mistakes excel.

Every business is about people and systems. Sometimes you need to have the wisdom to know what action to take. Other times you need to have the wisdom to not take action. Here's an example: at Starbucks every partner has an assigned position within the system. Each position has certain responsibilities. When everyone focuses on their responsibilities, and doing them as well as they can, then the store operates smoothly – just how it was designed. However, when one partner breaks the system and starts performing the responsibilities of others the system begins to breakdown.

It's the economic law of diminishing marginal returns. Having one or two people making beverages is the optimal scenario. Having four people trying to make beverages at the same time just becomes chaotic. You need to be wise enough to do less.

Other times you need to be wise enough to ask for help. This is one of the most common flaws, especially in very skilled baristas, and it goes back to pride. Check it at the door.

Many times a partner will get behind on their tasks when it's really busy. Maybe they have a lot of drinks sitting in queue but they don't want to ask for help.

It's true that many times they probably can catch up on their own, but at what cost? Customer wait time might go from two to five minutes. Maybe it only goes from two to three minutes. In the former scenario a customer goes from feeling like they had quick service to feeling like things were a little slow. Only one customer has to wait five minutes for it to impact the store negatively. In the latter example a customer goes from feeling like they just received exceptionally quick service to receiving just adequate service. By not asking for help the barista inadvertently set in motion a negative series of events.

It's not always easy to discern these scenarios but you need to anticipate them and learn from them when they do occur. You need to be wise enough to realize that it's not about your performance but the performance of the store that matters most. Partners that can do this on a regular basis are usually the top performers in the store. Candidates who can communicate this ability must be close to getting themselves hired.

Team player

If any phrase is cliché, it's "team player." Being a team player means a lot of different things. It means always trying to do what is best for the store, as we just discussed in the previous section. It means helping your fellow partners, knowing your role, and being versatile. It's doing what it takes to help the team succeed.

Doing what is best for the store isn't always easy. Sometimes the best thing can be hard to recognize. To recognize it you need to re-shape your paradigm. That means when you're about to perform a task ask yourself, "What is the best thing for the store?" You'll begin to train yourself to think like that and you'll be surprised with the answers you find.

You also need to be willing to help your fellow partners when they're struggling. Don't just watch while they struggle and think about how you're better than them. Help by coaching them to perform better. That might mean showing them how to make a beverage correctly or teaching them to think differently in a particular situation. Either way, if you're helping another partner get better then you're helping the team get better. People like that have a much greater impact on the store than those who only worry about themselves. When the team gets better, the store gets better.

Just as a football team can't operate if everyone wants to play quarterback, a Starbucks store can't operate if everyone is trying to run the cash register or make drinks. It's the supervisor's responsibility to ensure that everyone knows their role. It's each individual's responsibility to perform that role. Sound familiar? When a team player is attempting to make a wise decision they ask themselves: "What does the team need?"

This concept is easily lost in the busyness of a morning rush. Many times people act on instinct. They see something that needs to be done so they rush to do it. That doesn't usually work. You need to keep your role and not stray from it, lest you be needed in your primary role and not be there. Not sure? Ask.

A team player also needs to be versatile. Many times a partner is afraid to learn a new skill or position. Many times a partner only wants to work, or work hard, at their favorite position or task. If you're incapable or unwilling to fill a role that the team needs then how can you be a team player? This all goes back to the question: "What is the best thing for the store?" You need to master all tasks and be willing to perform them when they're needed. You don't have to be the best at every task but you need to be able to perform every task when your number is called. To put it another way, you don't have to be Kobe Bryant but you need to be Kobe for ten minutes if that's what the team needs.

Versatility encompasses two things: willingness and skillfulness. Are you willing to perform any task that is asked of you? If so, are you able to perform that task well? Will you, and can you, make drinks, get pastries, work in the drive-thru, clean the bathrooms, unpack the delivery, intelligently recommend coffee, work mornings and evenings, participate in community events, and train someone? The list can go on almost endlessly. The point is that people who are more versatile are more valuable to the store.

Multitasking

One of the essential skills needed to succeed at Starbucks is multitasking. If you've ever been a customer when it was busy, then you've probably seen it in action. A lot of tasks need to be performed in a finite amount of time. Being a proficient multitasker will ensure that they're completed in a timely manner.

Everyone believes that they're a great multitasker. They cite the fact that they have kids or that they've worked in a restaurant. They offer this as proof positive that they have great multitasking skills. That may very well be the case in their respective experiences. However, prior to Starbucks I was a restaurant manager and worked in restaurants for years. Multitasking in a restaurant and multitasking in a Starbucks are very different.

There are just so many things that need to be done in the span of a minute. From what I can see the most applicable work experience, as far as multitasking goes, is bartending. If you've bartended in a busy bar then you're multitasking skills are probably up to snuff.

People often cite prior coffee shop experience to justify their competency. But most coffee shops either lack the complexity (remember that at Starbucks you're making drinks from scratch) or the volume of customers to replicate the multitasking that is needed at Starbucks.

It's always said that women are better multitaskers than men. While I do have a bias, I'm not sold on that. It may very well be true on the aggregate but when I'm looking at a prospective employee I'm only looking at the individual. The two most efficient multi-taskers I ever worked with were both male. That's why people should be taken one at a time.

If you're not very strong at multitasking you can get better. You need to know what takes priority and then be quick to accomplish the tasks that you have prioritized. Master the tasks. Learn the priorities. Repeat the tasks according to prioritization.

Don't oversell your multitasking abilities. You might be fully capable of performing the job of barista at a high level but if you gush over yourself then you'll only come off as disingenuous or arrogant. Nobody wants either one. Instead of just praising your abilities communicate your understanding of how multitasking works. The interviewer isn't taking your praises at face value.

Coachability

If you want to work at Starbucks then you have to be coachable. It's imperative to being a strong partner. I don't know anyone that knows everything but I do know a lot of people that think they know everything. People like that don't fit well at Starbucks.

Being coachable doesn't just mean that you allow someone to train you, nor does it end when your training does. Being coachable means allowing someone else, namely your manager or supervisor, to advise and direct your skills and actions. It's an unending process.

Your manager sees the whole store more clearly than you do. Their role puts them in a better position. They can more readily see what is going well and what needs to be corrected within the store. This applies to supervisors as well. They're also in a good position to coach. If they're experienced then they have probably witnessed, a thousand times over, what works and what doesn't. When they see something that isn't working they'll try to fix it. This often involves coaching.

You have to be coachable no matter what position you're applying for. Baristas need to allow supervisors to coach them just as store managers need to allow district managers to coach them.

People don't like change and they don't like hearing that they aren't doing something as well as it can be done. I know, it seems impossible that someone could have a better application to your work than you do, but trust me there are always things that you can do better. Baristas and store managers alike don't like being coached and many times will flat out refuse to change or try something new. That mindset doesn't work. You can only get so far before crashing into the sun.

Being coachable is a very difficult thing to do. First, you need to accept that what you are doing might not be the optimal way. Again, I know, it's crazy. Second, you need to accept that you might be blind to the fact that what you are doing isn't the optimal way.

Lastly, and this may be the hardest part, you need to be willing to put forth a genuine effort to implement the new way. I can hear the groans now. "Ugh, why do we have to do this a new way? What's wrong with the old way?" Giving a genuine effort means setting aside pride and stubbornness and making repeated attempts. It doesn't mean trying it once and then saying that it doesn't work. If you only try it once then you really aren't trying. Stay committed to it for at least several weeks before assessing its effectiveness.

Actually doing these things is very difficult. You have to go outside of your comfort zone and try something new, something that might not be easy at first. It means trying it again and again. When someone is trying to coach you to change a specific behavior you have to stop to see how that new behavior will be more beneficial to the store. Ask yourself these questions: What am I doing? What is the new way of doing it? What are the benefits of the new way (How does it make the store better)? Seeing the benefits will give you the perspective that you need to change.

Every manager wants partners that are coachable. You need to mention it in the interview and then you need to be it when you get hired.

Positivity

You need to be positive. Not only does that mean having a "can-do" attitude, but it means not being negative. People love to be negative. It seems to be human nature. You need to be positive about yourself and those around you.

Legendary college basketball coach John Wooden said, "Don't whine, don't complain, don't make excuses. Just do the best you can. Nobody can do more than that." It applies to college basketball and it applies to the workplace. Besides, John Wooden won ten national championships so I listen carefully to what he says about attitude.

A defeatist attitude hardly ever wins the day. Being positive doesn't mean that you will be successful but you can't be successful without being positive.

Many times I have seen new partners get down on themselves during their first month or two at Starbucks. The issue is that the job entails a lot of learning, swiftness, and alacrity. These things can take time to master. Sometimes people who are very smart and capable quit because they haven't mastered their position as quickly as they would've liked. If they could've held on for another month or so they would've been fine. It's a job that takes time to learn. Keep that in mind.

On the other hand, you need to keep a positive attitude toward your coworkers and customers. Negativity toward your job and tasks can't be productive. It only erodes character and productivity. Poor treatment of a coworker is nothing but detrimental to the team and store. When it occurs, it almost always revolves around a partner who is a poor performer. Sometimes that poor performer is left to struggle because the others have given up on them. Other times it's a careless comment. These actions usually aren't intended to cause damage but do so nonetheless. All of these actions, along with those like them, rip at the fabric of the store. They begin to create poor attitudes that not only hurt the psyche of the partners but also store performance. It's a slippery slope that can snowball fast.

In addition to negativity there's gossip. Gossip is one of the most dangerous things to the well being of a store. It's also one of the hardest things to stop once it's been set in motion. You need to constantly be on guard for it. People regularly contribute to it unwittingly. How many times have you witnessed gossip do damage in the lives of others? In your life? It doesn't belong in the store.

You need to be in control of your attitude or others will control it for you. It's like we said earlier, a little bit of leaven goes through the whole dough. If you can maintain a truly positive attitude, and the right mindset, then you'll not only make yourself a better asset for the store but you'll make the store, and those around you, better.

Specialists

While we've discussed some skills that all partners need to possess there are some specialty skills that are applicable as well. These include sales, artistic ability, coffee knowledge, and general building maintenance skills. I found these particular skill sets to be invaluable in the store.

The first one is sales. It takes a special kind of person to be good at sales. You need to be knowledgeable about the product, have a strong pitch, be motivated to sell, and have thick skin for getting rejected. A lot of us don't possess all of those qualities. Those who do are incredibly valuable. The store regularly has sales goals that it needs to meet. It's regularly two or three people who carry the store to achieving those goals. If you have a selling skill then you need to make that clear when you apply.

Don't think you're the selling type? Don't sell yourself short just yet. (See, you're already a salesman. I love that line.) I've seen many people, that when put in that position, discover for the first time that they can sell. It's always a surprise to them and a huge confidence booster.

Artistic ability is another skill that's in demand. Each store has several chalkboard signs that need to be updated regularly in addition to small sales displays that also draw on artistic ability – no pun intended. It's a valuable skill but if the store already has three strong artists then your skill might not give you an advantage. You can never have enough salesmen but there are only so many chalkboards.

A partner with a passion for coffee is always great to have at the store. The manager usually has a lot of coffee knowledge and other partners are educated on coffee to a degree. However, none of these are substitutes for a partner who has a real passion for coffee at every point in the coffee process. They simply soak up more because they love it so much. That passion spills out during their workday. It's nice to have a couple partners with that level of coffee knowledge. My coffee knowledge is fairly deep but seldom did I ever work in a store without a partner who knew more about coffee than me. That partner, or partners, was a terrific resource so many times. It's definitely a valuable passion.

Lastly, if you have a handyman skill then I would make that known when you apply. I used to work with a man who could fix anything in the store that needed to be fixed. I don't mean he could just re-attach cabinet doors or construct shelving units. He could do anything that we needed done. So many times he offered to complete the construction projects that I was forced to use independent contractors for. What a waste of resources.

He was able to solve electrical issues, lay pipes, and provide professional level maintenance to all parts of the building. We worked in a building that used to be a bank. In the middle of our backroom was a huge vault with the door welded shut. We could've really used that space. I'll never forget the day that he offered to bring in a blowtorch and remove the several-ton door. As much as I would've loved to have that space I wasn't ready to take on that safety risk. But I know he could've done it. He contributed much more to the store than his maintenance and general building skills, but I often found those skills to be invaluable. If you can offer that, then you'll increase your chances of getting hired.

A Few More Skills...

Composure – Starbucks wants individuals who aren't going to scream and run out the front door when a little bit of adversity arises.

Ambiguity – Speaking of the unexpected, you need to be able to deal with it. Not only do many unexpected things happen, but oftentimes new company policies are implemented. Change, change, change.

Initiative – Step up to the plate and take the bull by the horns. That means taking responsibility for your own personal development and performing tasks before you are asked.

For Supervisors

Coaching – You need to be able to coach baristas' behaviors to fit the store's requirements and ambitions. Get to know each barista.

Leadership – The best thing you can do is lead by example. "Do as I say, not as I do" never works. It takes a great deal of maturity, resolve, and business knowledge (the business of the store) to do this.

Results – You need to have a plan for what you want to accomplish on your shift. This means preparation as well as staying informed about goals. Then you need to track progress and steer the ship.

For Managers

Leadership – It's imperative. It's more than just leading by example. It means being a servant to those you work with. It's consistent composure, decisiveness, moral uprightness, owning responsibility for your mistakes (which you're sure to have – large and small), candor (saying what needs to be said), planning and preparedness, problem resolution, preparing others, empowering others, having the courage to champion an unpopular idea, thick skin and much more. All of which is an ongoing learning process that you'll never be perfect at. I certainly took some on the chin.

Results – You need to get them. Not at all costs but you need to get them. Plan for them, communicate them, sell them to your team, and track them. Everyone is motivated by something so get to know what motivates your team members. Know your business well enough to know when to push your team to get results and when to back off so you don't overwork them.

Planning – Failure to plan is planning to fail. It's cliché but it's true. As much as you need to be able to handle ambiguity you need to prepare and plan for the known and the unknown. It's irresponsible not to. A good question to ask yourself when planning is, "What do I need to do to keep the store two steps ahead?"

Environment – Every partner plays their part in creating the environment of the store. However, you have the greatest influence. You need to shape it. Don't let others shape it for you. When you shape others they help you shape the store.

Development – You need to develop your partners for the next level. The more skilled a partner is then the better the store will be. Besides, you need to create a "bench" because you never know when a supervisor will quit or you'll be out on medical leave.

Organization – Be organized in everything that you do. Some of my lowest moments were when I became unorganized.

Store – Aside from ethics and safety, the store is number one. If it's ethical and moral then the question should always be "What is the best decision for the store?" Answering that question helps you keep perspective and usually gives you answers. It might give you tough answers but it'll help keep you on track.

Consistently maintaining all of these qualities is impossible. Since your actions permeate the store, you do need to be able to identify when you're lacking somewhere so that you can take corrective action. However, if you don't know where to look, then you won't be able to indentify it.

Conclusion

If you want to get hired at Starbucks then you need to exhibit a majority of the attributes and skills that I've listed here. They're vital whether you want to be a barista, supervisor, or manager.

Also, I think honesty and ethics goes without saying. Many people purport to be honest but when their honesty is tried they fail. All of us fail at times but you can always pick out those who are striving to be honest. They're forthcoming with information that is detrimental to them and they give you their true feelings when they disagree with you.

It takes courage to be honest. I once worked with a guy who confessed to me that he'd stolen. He was someone who was generally honest but made a mistake. Nevertheless, it took courage to admit that since he knew he would lose his job. Honesty is so, so underrated.

You might also be wondering how experience plays into the fold. I've never felt that experience was a deciding factor for the barista position. Plenty of people who apply have coffee shop experience and they seem no more likely to be a good barista than someone who doesn't. I usually found their experience to be overrated.

Those who have been previously employed by Starbucks, or who want to transfer from one store to another, obviously have an edge. That's only because they know the technical skills of the job. In my experience, I have found that many of them probably weren't as effective in their previous store as I would like them to be in mine. So while they enjoy a bit of an advantage over those without Starbucks experience I would still tread lightly. The advantage of hiring someone without that experience is that you, as a manager, get to mold them. I always preferred that. If you don't have experience, then tell the interviewer that you're "moldable." It's a good point that might garner a chuckle as well.

People also like to stereotype. They believe that a middle-aged person is mature and responsible but not quick or adept at multitasking. The opposite stereotype is believed by many as well. That is, young kids are not mature or responsible, yet they'll be quick. I've found neither of those stereotypes to be that accurate. I've worked with responsible seventeen-year-olds, immature forty-year-olds, strong fifty-year-old multitaskers, slow twenty-two-year-olds, and some really slow teenagers. So, you take applicants one at a time. Everyone is different.

I've also found that recommendations don't mean a whole lot. Most of the candidates that were recommended to me didn't work out. Be that as it may, you're more likely to get hired with a good recommendation.

The only constants are the skills that are needed to excel at the job. When interviewing you should strive to communicate your proficiency in the characteristics I have described. They're what will make you a good candidate, what will get you hired, and what will help you succeed.

Chapter Nine:

Kids' Drinks

"I have found the best way to give advice to your children is to find out what they want and then advise them to do it."
– Harry S. Truman

B elow I have compiled a list of popular kids' drinks. Hopefully you'll find it of some use when you're trying to decide on a beverage for your child.

Please note that hot kids' drinks are not steamed to the same temperature as adult drinks. They're steamed to about 130°F. A hot kids' drink is served in an 8 oz. cup, while a kids' iced or Frappuccino drink is served in a 12 oz. cup. All of the listed drinks are decaffeinated.

1. Organic Chocolate Milk

This is probably the most popular kids' drink that Starbucks offers. You can get it from the refrigerated display. It comes in a carton with a straw. Chocolate milk can also be made at the bar.

2. Organic Vanilla Milk

Sweet vanilla milk. It's available in the refrigerated display and comes in a carton with a straw. Vanilla milk can also be made at the bar.

3. Apple Juice Box

This is located in the refrigerated display by the register. It's packaged in a carton with a straw. If there aren't any then you can ask for apple juice poured at the bar. You also have the option of steaming it (Steamed Apple Juice) if it's poured from the bar.

4. Hot Chocolate

It contains chocolate, vanilla, 2% milk and whip. White hot chocolate and Salted Caramel Hot Chocolate are also available.

5. Vanilla Crème

It's just vanilla syrup, steamed 2% milk and whip.

6. Caramel Apple Spice

This is a great warm apple beverage. It contains cinnamon dolce syrup, apple juice, whip, and caramel sauce. Kids love it.

7. Strawberries and Crème Frappuccino

It's a sweet frozen strawberry drink. It's great on a hot day. You can ask for less Classic syrup and no whip if you want to make it lighter.

8. Double Chocolaty Chip Frappuccino

It's good if your kid likes chocolate and chocolate chips. Adding peppermint is a nice modification.

9. Vanilla Bean Frappuccino

If your kid likes vanilla milkshakes or vanilla crèmes then they will probably like this. It's a good alternative to chocolate.

10. Blended Strawberry Lemonade

This should be way more popular with kids than it is. It simply isn't well known. Lemonade and strawberry purée, blended together with some sweetener, has to be good.

11. Passion Iced Tea Lemonade

This is a decaffeinated fruity tea with lemonade and sweetener.

12. Pumpkin Spice Crème

If your kid likes pumpkin, and it's the fall, then you can get them a Pumpkin Spice Crème. It's just steamed milk, sweet pumpkin flavor, and whip.

Chapter Ten:

Odds and Ends

"I'm not confused, I'm just well mixed." – Robert Frost

Some information is pertinent, but it doesn't really fit in anywhere. That's what this section is for. I hope you find it helpful.

- If you're not sure about what you want to order, or if you want to try something new, then you can ask for a sample. You can sample almost anything in the store, especially handcrafted beverages and pastries.

- Every now and then a kind drive-thru customer will pay for the car behind them simply because they want to be nice. They didn't even know them. It made the recipient's day every time.

- Many stores display artwork by local artists. If you're an artist you should check with your local Starbucks for openings.

- Many stores love to have events. An art gallery, entertainment (music, balloon artist, magician), poetry/book reading, and community fundraisers are all things that a lot of stores will welcome. If you have something to offer you may want to inquire.

- Some Starbucks have hosted birthday parties. They stay open an hour late, or close an hour early, on their slowest night, give the birthday boy/girl an apron, and train them to make drinks. They make drinks for the rest of the birthday party. This may take some schmoozing, particularly with the regional office, but you can pull it off.

- Do you collect Starbucks city mugs? If you are looking for a city in the current collection you might be able to have your local Starbucks order it for you. If not, calling or writing Starbucks stores in, and around, that city is another option. If they have it they can ship it to you. If not, there's always eBay.

- If you're looking for any retail items: mugs, cups, tumblers, or Bearistas you can probably have your local Starbucks order it for you. They can also tell you if a nearby store has what you're looking for. It's only a phone call away if the store can't obtain it through its normal ordering process. Usually, an item can be ordered unless it's out of stock at the distribution center.

- Starbucks stores are either company owned or licensed. They aren't traditional franchises like other companies in the industry. Most stores are company owned and operated. Generally, stores in Target, Barnes and Noble, Marriott, and airports, are licensed and operated by those companies and organizations. You should take them on a case-by-case basis but from what I know you'll get better service, and have a better all-around experience, at company operated stores. Just my opinion.

- If you want to get a treat for your dog then order whipped cream in a short cup. They love it!

- Have a green thumb? You can get free coffee grounds from your local Starbucks through the Grounds for Gardens program. Stores have a designated bucket with bags of free grounds. If you don't see it just ask them to save some for you. I'm sure they'll be happy to.

- If your regular drink doesn't taste right, or if you simply don't like the new drink you're trying, make sure you speak up. You're entitled to a new one.

- I know there are many customers interested in purchasing espresso machines. Starbucks used to sell them. They were discontinued not long ago. I've never found the fully automatic, uber-expensive, machines to be anything special. The maintenance and cleaning was too much. I believe the manual machines have better value. I've always recommended the Starbucks Barista, Saeco Via Venezia, or similar machines. I used to have a Venezia. It's not automatic but it has far fewer variables and is easy to maintain. You can't replace the Verismo and Mastrena industrial machines that Starbucks stores use but the drinks taste good. Also, buy espresso pods and save yourself a mess.

- If you're simply looking for a coffee maker then you might want to try a Keurig. They're all the rage. Looking to spend less money? I've been using a Mr. Coffee machine for years. It works just fine.

- Every store offers porcelain cups. If you're planning to stay in the store then ask for your drink in porcelain. It tastes better and saves paper.

- Starbucks does offer a customer rewards program. It is ever evolving but usually contains free add-ons (syrup, soy milk), free drinks, and coupons. If you're at least a semi-regular customer you should sign up. If you don't you're missing out on free stuff. Check with your local store for the latest on the program.

- After all of those frustrating years Starbucks Wi-Fi is now free and simple to use. Just open your browser, agree to the terms of service, and you're in.

- If you're involved in a nonprofit or community activity that is in need of food, coffee, or raffle donations then Starbucks is a prospect for you. It's very difficult to solicit a cash donation but if you need coffee for an event, a basket of goodies for a raffle, or food for your shelter or soup kitchen then you need to be in touch with your local Starbucks. There's a good chance they'll be able to help.

Lastly, I'd like to discuss some nutritional information. As a society we have become evermore conscious about the gluten, peanut, dairy, and corn syrup content of the food and beverages that we consume. While these contents are ever changing, in the consumer friendly direction, at Starbucks below is my take as of early 2012. As a first rule always ask the barista for the latest information.

Gluten. If you have celiac disease then you not only take issue with gluten but you're also not alone among the Starbucks customer base. A lot of people ask for gluten free products. Here's what I can tell you: Starbucks will never state, and rightfully so, that any non-prepackaged food or drink item is gluten-free, dairy free or whatever free because of the possibility of cross contamination.

Pastries, as you probably imagine, are pretty much out. They all contain gluten with one caveat: Starbucks has tested from time to time a packaged gluten-free pastry in their pastry cases. They've never had staying power and have always been pulled. The pastry case isn't the first place you should look but they'll probably keep experimenting so keep your eyes open.

Snacks are where you'll find gluten-free food. At the counter and in the retail display baskets Starbucks has continuously added gluten-free products and they've sold well, very well. They've stayed. These products have changed from time to time but have included:

- Kind Bars - all varieties

- Peeled Snacks - a few different flavors

- Lucy Cookies

- Two Mom's in the Raw bars

- Food Should Taste Good chips (the sweet potato ones are really good)

- There are also some fruit snacks.

With drinks you have to be careful because there is the possibility of cross contamination. With that said, coffees, teas, and espresso drinks should be ok. I would question the syrups because some ingredients on the labels are generalized.

Peanuts. The pastry case is ripe for cross contamination. Even if none of the pastries have peanuts many are made in the same facilities as those that do.

I've never seen peanut butter anything as a drink component. Nevertheless, since there are pastries ten feet away, cross contamination is still possible no matter how unlikely it may seem.

Corn Syrup. Starbucks dumped it a few years ago so I doubt they would bring it back. None of the syrups have it.

Dairy. If it's a drink that's normally made with milk it can always be made with soy. All of the syrups should be ok with one exception: chocolate/white chocolate. I would ask the barista for the package to double check. Frappuccinos used to use a syrup with dairy but not anymore. I'm sure there's milk in the chocolate chips.

The biggest concern is human error. There are milk and Frappuccino pitchers designated for non-dairy beverages. I've also seen dairy put into them. The baristas get training but there are a lot of small details that they might not absorb. Most people want to do the right thing, and I'm not saying it's the norm, but with thousands of stores and baristas it's a fact that mistakes happen.

Remember, you're dealing with a human element. If you're concerned you can confirm with the barista when you receive your drink that it's dairy free. Or you can even ask them sanitize the pitcher before making your beverage.

Glossary

affogato: (ah-feh-gah-tō) Italian word that means *drowned*. It refers to the process of pouring an espresso shot on top of a drink instead of mixing it in.

Americano: See *Caffè Americano*.

barista: (ba-ree-stuh) Italian for *bartender*. It's someone who serves espresso-based beverages.

black eye: Drip coffee with two shots of espresso added to it.

black tie: Refers to a mocha or hot chocolate that incorporates both milk chocolate and white chocolate.

bold: Term generally used to refer to coffees with a bolder flavor. The term *bold* is an adjective for flavor and not a reference to the caffeine content. That's a common misunderstanding.

breve: (brev-ey) Refers to steamed half-and-half. Generally steamed espresso beverages are made with milk. Substituting that milk with half-and-half would make it a breve beverage.

café: (kaf-ey) French word for coffee. In the U.S. it generally refers to a coffee shop.

café au lait: (kaf-ey ō ley) French phrase for *coffee with milk*. This normally refers to a beverage that is half drip coffee and half steamed milk. Starbucks sells this beverage under the title Caffè Misto, which is Italian.

caffè: (kaf-ey) Italian for coffee.

Caffè Americano: (kaf-ey uh-mer-i-kan-ō) Can also be *Café Americano.* Means *American Coffee.* It's a beverage comprised of espresso and water (hot or cold). It has its origin in the European Theater of World War 2. Americans ordering espresso would add water so it was more to their liking. That is, like the coffee back in the U.S.

Caffè Latte: (kaf-ey lah-tey) Can also be *Café Latte.* It means *coffee* [and] *milk.* It refers to a beverage made with espresso and steamed milk.

Caffè Misto: (kaf-ey mee-stō) Can also be *Café Misto.* This term means *coffee mixed.* It refers to a beverage that is half drip coffee and half steamed milk; the same thing as a café au lait.

Caffè Mocha: (kaf-ey mō-ka) Can also be *Café Mocha.* This refers to a beverage made with espresso, steamed milk, chocolate, and in the Starbucks sense, whipped cream. It's purely an American drink. You would be hard pressed to find it in Europe outside of an American establishment. The term *mocha* is generally used to refer to a mixture of coffee and chocolate flavors.

Cappuccino: (kap-oo-chee-nō) Beverage made with espresso and foamy milk. When the steamed milk settles you'll usually find that you have a drink consisting of equal parts milk and foam mixed with espresso. The term literally means *small cap.*

Caramel Macchiato: (mahk-ee-ah-tō) Refers to a beverage that is made with vanilla flavoring, espresso, steamed milk, milk foam, and caramel sauce. Macchiato means *marked.* It's a layered drink where the espresso shots are going into the drink last instead of first, thus marking the top of the drink with a brown dot.

con panna: (con pahn-ah) Italian term that means *with cream.* Specifically, it refers to whipped cream.

crema: (kre-mah) Top layer of an espresso shot. Should be reddish brown in color and have a caramelly sweet flavor.

demitasse: (dem-i-tahs) French term for *half cup.* It refers to the tiny little cups that espresso is served in.

doppio: (dō-pee-ō) Italian for *double.* It refers to two shots, or two ounces, of espresso. Simply say *doppio* when ordering only two shots of espresso.

double: Refers to two shots of espresso.

drizzle: As we like to say in the biz: *drizz.* It's a reference to the sauce that is drizzled on top of some beverages. Available flavors are usually chocolate and caramel.

dry: A modification for milk, usually cappuccinos. It means more foam, or in the case of a cappuccino, more foam than milk. So, if that's how you prefer your cappuccino, mostly foam, then you should order it *dry.* If you like it almost all foam then order it *extra dry* or *bone dry.*

espresso: (es-pres-ō) Sometimes colloquially pronounced *ex-press-ō.* It refers to both a drink and a brewing method. In the former it's concentrated coffee that comes in one ounce servings. The latter refers to hot water being forced through very finely ground coffee. It's enjoyed for its rich taste, crema (foam), and high concentration of caffeine.

espresso con panna; (es-pres-ō con pahn-ah) A beverage that consists of espresso with whipped cream on top. It translates *espresso with cream*.

espresso macchiato: (es-pres-ō mahk-ee-ah-tō) A beverage consisting of espresso with milk foam on top. It translates *marked espresso*.

Frappuccino: (frap-uh-chee-nō) An exclusive Starbucks frozen beverage.

French press: A coffee lover's preferred brewing method. Coarsely ground coffee soaks in hot water for four minutes. The soaking contributes to richer and more distinct flavors. By contrast, in traditional drip brewing methods, the water has less contact time with the grounds because it is passing through and not sitting around them.

grande: (grahn-day) Often mispronounced *gran-dee* or *grand*. It's Italian for *large* and refers to the 16 oz. medium size offered at Starbucks.

latte: See *Caffé Latte*.

London Fog: Slang for an Earl Grey tea latte. An Earl Grey tea latte consists of vanilla flavoring, Earl Grey tea, hot water, steamed milk, and milk foam.

long: Refers to an espresso brewing method. If you ask for a long espresso then you will get espresso that has had about twice as much water pushed through the grounds, thus resulting in a larger quantity of diluted espresso. It also takes about twice as long to pour. When compared to regular shots of espresso long shots are weaker in flavor and more bitter. The Italian for long is *lungo*. *Café lungo* is also an accurate variation of the term.

macchiato: (mahk-ee-ah-tō) Literally means *marked*. For the beverage description see *espresso macchiato* or *Caramel Macchiato*.

melted: Refers to the process of melting raw sugar in a beverage before completing it. Raw sugar is coarser than other sugars and doesn't mix well on its own, particularly in iced beverages. So, if you prefer raw sugar and you would like it mixed into your beverage better, ask that it be melted with some hot water before the rest of the components are added.

mild: Adjective that refers to the potency of a coffee's flavor. Coffees without very poignant flavors are often referred to as mild.

Misto: (mee-stō) See *Café Misto*.

mocha: (mō-kah) Refers to the blending of coffee and chocolate flavors. For the beverage definition see *Caffé Mocha*.

partner: Anyone who is employed by Starbucks. All employees are considered partners because of the company's stock grants.

quad: Four shots of espresso.

red eye: A beverage that consists of drip coffee with one shot of espresso added to it.

ristretto: (ris-tret-ō) An espresso brewing method that is the converse of the long method. It's a short shot of espresso that's created by pushing less water through the coffee grounds than when making a standard shot. It's a bolder and less bitter shot of espresso.

room: Term used to leave space in the cup. This is usually for adding milk but sometimes to simply prevent spillage while traveling.

short: Smallest size at Starbucks – 8 oz. to be exact.

single: Term used when you only want one shot of espresso in your beverage.

skinny: Term that references drinks that contain non-fat milk, sugar-free syrup, and lack whipped cream.

sleeve: The paper holder that slips around the cup so you don't burn your hand.

splash stick: Little green sticks that plug the opening in the cup lids. They not only keep the drink from spilling but they also help keep it warmer for a longer period of time.

Starbucks experience: The experience of going into a Starbucks and getting the drink that you want, with friendly service, and in a welcoming atmosphere.

tall: The small size cup that Starbucks offers – 12 oz. It's not the smallest size – that's short – but the small size. Tall is small.

third place: Your first place is your home, your second place is where you work, your third place is where you meet with family and friends. It's where you congregate to enjoy each other and share stories, where you relax, read the paper, daydream, and get away. Starbucks strives to be that place.

trenta: (tren-tah) It means *thirty* in Italian. It's the extra large, 31 oz. size. Only iced coffee and tea are available in this size.

triple: Three shots of espresso.

upside down: A modification that's usually applied to a Caramel Macchiato. A Caramel Macchiato is usually made with the espresso shots and the caramel sauce being applied last. When ordered upside down they're applied first. This is desirable because it mixes both into the drink, especially the caramel, instead of allowing them to sit on top. This is even more applicable when the Caramel Macchiato is iced.

venti: (ven-tee) The large size – 24 oz.

VIA: (vee-uh) Ready-brew coffee that Starbucks sells. It's a micro-grind that dissolves instantly into water and milk.

wet: A modification that's mostly applied to cappuccinos. Cappuccinos generally contain equal parts milk and milk foam. If you want more milk than milk foam then you'll order it *wet*. If you want mostly milk then you should order it *extra wet*.

INDEX

A

B

C

N

nutmeg, 95

O

oolong tea, 59
Orange Blossom tea, 64
Orange Mango Smoothie, 181-182
ordering, 189-191
Organic Yukon Blend, 55-56

P

pairing, 46-47, 50-58
partner, 233
Passion Iced Tea, 64, 139-140
Passion Iced Tea Lemonade, 64, 139-140
Passion tea, 64, 139-140
peanut, 227-228
peppermint, 82-83
Peppermint Mocha, 147-148
Peppermint Mocha Frappuccino, 178-180
percolator, 40
Pike Place Roast, 47, 56
powders, 90-92
proportion, 43
protein and fiber powder, 90-91
pumpkin spice, 82-83, 95
Pumpkin Spice Latte, 149-150

R

S

Z